Bankers in the Selling Role

Bankers in the Selling Role

A CONSULTATIVE GUIDE TO CROSS-SELLING FINANCIAL SERVICES

LINDA RICHARDSON

Second Edition

A Wiley-Interscience Publication
JOHN WILEY & SONS
New York • Chichester • Brisbane • Toronto • Singapore

Library of Congress Cataloging in Publication Data:

Richardson, Linda
  Bankers in the selling role.

  "A Wiley-Interscience publication."
  Includes index.
  1. Bank marketing.   I. Title.

HG1616.M3R53   1984   332.1′068′8   84–11937
ISBN 0-471-81005-3

Printed in the United States of America

10 9 8 7 6 5 4 3 2

To
my mother and father
with gratitude and love

Preface

The concepts in this book have been drawn directly from the experience of more than 1000 bankers ranging from senior management and bank officers to management trainees. Observations from the field as well as from sales seminars provided evidence that contradicted the old adage that "salespeople are born, not made."

By utilizing the consultative selling process described here, bankers who did not think that they had a predilection—much less a talent—for selling developed confidence and achieved success in their new selling roles. They used their product knowledge and selling skills to individualize their sales calls, meet the needs of their customers, and generate positive sales action. In short, they *sold,* and at the same time they developed long-term relationships that were beneficial to the customer and the bank.

The objectives of this book are to create an awareness and acceptance of the role of sales in banking and to help bankers plan and conduct effective sales interviews.

The consultative approach to sales in banking presented in this book is designed to assist bankers in their roles as financial consultants to their customers and to provide them with an approach to sales that is suitable for the relationship that exists between bankers and customers. It provides bankers with an alternative to "hard," "door-to-door" or product-driven selling.

One of the most common concerns expressed by bankers about selling is their desire to avoid anything that resembles the hard sell. Although they reject the idea of hard selling, many untrained bankers who are placed in selling situations often resort to hard-sell tactics simply because they think that is what selling is all about.

This is not so. Hard selling is *product* selling rather than *need* selling. Hard selling is "hard" in its approach *and* in its wear and tear on customers and bankers alike. During a hard sell, customers are often looking for a way out, and bankers are searching for a way in: Often bankers recite their laundry lists of products, searching for a spark of interest from the customer, who is interested in nothing more than concluding the sales interview. The antithesis of hard selling is consultative selling. By identifying customer needs and understanding the customer's situation *before* selling a product, bankers are better able to avoid the hard-sell trap. By understanding their products from their customer's point of view, they are better able to relate the products to their customer's needs. Customers buy benefits, not features; they buy solutions, not products. Consultative selling helps bankers understand customer needs and utilize the features and benefits of their products to respond to those needs and expand relationships.

Consultative banking recognizes that product knowledge is the cornerstone of selling. The consultative approach to selling helps bankers understand and communicate the product advantages that respond to a customer's competitive situation. Indeed, it is the banker's ability to discuss a product relative to the customer's needs within the marketplace that differentiates products that are basically competitive.

The competitive advantage lies not so much in the operations or features of a basically competitive product as in the banker's understanding of the product and how it compares to that of the competition, and the banker's skill in relating the value of the product to the customer's needs. If a product is basically competitive, bankers can gain a disproportionately high share of the market by using the consultative sales approach. By communicating sales-oriented product information in a consultative manner, bankers can create their own marketing edge over their competitors.

Among bank products, there appear to be striking similarities. Upon closer examination, however, bank products differ significantly in features and benefits, qualifying criteria, operational and implementation procedures, personal service, and overall design. For example, for a product as common as Lock Box, one bank may have 15 pickups daily as compared to five by another bank, thus gaining quicker processing. One bank may have a minimum of 1000 items for a customer to qualify as a prospect for Lock Box, and another bank may require only 250 items. One bank may have an automated system and another a manual system. Surely, there are no perfect products, and there are very few, if any, identical products among banks.

Bankers can differentiate their products from those of others by being able to understand and discuss them from the customer's point of view relative to the customer's situation. Customers are continuously evaluating products, asking, ''What's in it for me?'' Consultative banking helps bankers answer that question for credit, noncredit, and credit-related products or services. Consultative banking also benefits bankers since it provides them with a way to develop long-term, loyal relationships that are mutually beneficial to the customer and the bank.

Although the concepts in this book have been shaped by the sales experience of more than 1000 bankers, the pages of the book cannot replace individual experience. Rather, the consultative sales approach is aimed at accelerating the mastery that comes with experience. Being effective in sales does not have to be learned the hard way, by trial and error. The goal of the book is to increase bankers' willingness to initiate sales by developing the information, skills, and attitudes they need to be confident in their selling roles. It offers them a framework they can use to assess their sales effectiveness, improve their post-sales-call evaluation, and recover during a call. By understanding the sales process and having a flexible framework for controlling the sales interview, bankers can accelerate their effectiveness and enjoy selling.

Linda Richardson

Philadelphia, Pennsylvania
July 1984

Acknowledgments

I am grateful to all of the professionals with whom I have worked, who have shared their knowledge and experience with me. I extend special thanks to my friend and colleague Dannie O'Connor for her support and encouragement, to my teachers Juanita Kidd Stout, Albert Ellis, and Marc Bassin for their patience and guidance, and to Charlie McCabe and John Conde at Manufacturers Hanover Trust for their vision of the role of sales in banking and their support of my initial efforts. I am also indebted to thousands of bankers and their banks for their invaluable contributions, without which this book could not exist.

L. R.

Contents

1 An Introduction to Consultative Banking   1

Sales in Banking, 2
Resistance to Selling, 3
Image of Selling, 4
Sales Role of Bankers, 5

2 Product Knowledge   9

Product Knowledge as the Foundation of Selling, 10
Sales-Oriented Product Knowledge, 11
Resources for Product Knowledge, 12
*Twenty-three Critical Product Knowledge Categories
    for a Sales Interview,* 14
Sales Line, 28
Product Knowledge Questions, 29
Tying Product Knowledge to Customer Needs, 34
Summary, 37

3 Consultative Sales Approach   39

Ten Elements of a Sales Interview, 40
Preparing for the Sales Call, 110
Declining a Transaction, 113
Joint Calling, 114
Sales with Two or More Customers, 116
Managing the Decision-Making Unit, 125
Sales Materials, 128

4   Aspects of Developing and Managing Relationships   **133**

Prospecting, 134
The Telephone as a Relationship Management Tool, 147
Nurturing the Account, 149

5   Sales Tips   **155**

Possible Difficulties, 164

6   Self-Training for Line Bankers   **167**

Reader's Feedback Summary   **171**

Index   **173**

1
An Introduction to Consultative Banking

SALES IN BANKING

Consultative banking recognizes the importance of the role of sales in banking. Bankers are required to initiate business, to cross-sell, and to function as consultants to their customers if they expect to achieve a fair or disproportionately high share of the market.

Consultative banking is an approach to sales that provides bankers with the skills required to increase market share profitably and develop long-term relationships in a highly competitive environment. It provides bankers with an approach for understanding the bank's noncredit as well as credit products, a process for identifying customer needs and leading effective sales interviews, and a planning and follow-up system. Consultative banking focuses on the sales communication process between bankers and customers, helping bankers look at their products and services from the customer's point of view. It appreciates the value that the customer derives from the sale. It is the antithesis of door-to-door selling, since the needs of individual customers are the focal point of the sale. Bankers who use the consultative approach can recognize and maximize opportunities by discussing alternatives with customers and assisting them in making decisions with confidence.

Consultative banking is a process for planning, implementing, and nurturing a relationship. It provides bankers with tools they need to link their bank's capabilities with their customer's situation and increase their ability to uncover needs, solve problems, and improve situations.

Consultative banking aims at building long-term relations that are beneficial to both the customer and the bank. Bankers must conclude sales that are not only in the best interests of the bank, protecting its profit margin, but also in the best interests of the customer. Mutually beneficial relationships should be the rule, not the exception.

The following case history illustrates a mutually beneficial sale.

Background. A company that was a customer of the bank had a check-processing system with numerous problems, such as incorrect serial numbers, lost checks, and late processing.

Bank Intervention. A banker became aware of the company's problem during a follow-up call and arranged a meeting with the product specialist from the cash management unit to discuss the problem. During the joint call, the product specialist introduced the idea of a special indexing process in which the customer could save time, reduce costs, and reduce problems. The customer agreed to try the new system.

Analysis. The banker's objective for the follow-up call was to discuss the customer's cash flow needs. The banker was able to apply his product knowledge when a problem surfaced. By calling in the product specialist to discuss cash management capabilities, not only were the customer's problems solved but the bank's internal marketing objective of converting customers from regular sorting to special indexing was also achieved. Both the customer and the bank were able to reduce costs and save time. By satisfying a customer's needs and correcting a problem, the banker nurtured and strengthened a valued relationship. The bank was able to increase the cost by 3¢ per item (over 30%). The customer was so satisfied with the efficiency of the new system that he converted one other company account and sought cash management consultation for his headquarters.

In this example, the banker applied his product knowledge to a customer's need. By striving for a mutually beneficial arrangement, he satisfied the need and succeeded in cross-selling a product enhancement. (The term *cross-selling* means providing additional bank products or services to current customers.) The banker discussed the product from the customer's perspective, pointing out the benefits that would accrue to the customer with the new system. At the same time, the banker promoted the bank's interests.

RESISTANCE TO SELLING

Although the consultative approach to sales in banking affords bankers the opportunity to serve as advisers and consultants to their customers, not all bankers are comfortable with the idea of selling. Selling appears to many bankers to be a departure from the profession they originally selected. Previously, bankers had, at best, passive selling roles in which they waited for business to walk in the door. But in today's highly competitive environment, bank managements throughout the country have redefined bankers' roles and now include in their primary responsibilities active sales solicitation as a part of relationship management. The change from reactive to proactive selling has been stimulated by aggressive marketing from within the banking industry, competition from nonbanking institutions, inroads by foreign banks, new technology, deregulation, sophisticated cash management in corporations, and a changing loan environment. The keen competitive environment has caused the senior management of both regional and money-center banks to emphasize the sale of noncredit and credit-related products in their marketing plans as a way to develop, expand, and protect relationships. Bankers who chose banking as a "non-selling" profession are now caught in the transition.

Many bankers, both new and experienced, find it hard to reconcile the apparent contradiction that has surfaced in their profession. Many resist selling basically because they think that all selling is high pressure. As long as they associate sales with high-pressure tactics and misrepresentations, they will correctly reject it as unprofessional and unworthy of banking.

Fortunately, not all selling is high-pressure or disreputable. Consultative selling is the antithesis of high-pressure sales. Perhaps by differentiating the various kinds of selling, it will be possible to isolate the negative image and contrast it with the positive benefits that can accrue to customers and bankers alike through consultative selling.

IMAGE OF SELLING

A look at the image of selling over the past century may shed some light on the stigma sometimes associated with sales. From the beginning, the image of sales in this country was in serious trouble. The "snake-oil" salesman dominated selling in the 1800s. He was a charismatic individual, and as an entertainer or "healer" he charmed a naive and gullible public with his dramatizations. His monologue was filled with exaggerated claims. He was the quintessential con artist or flimflam man, traveling from town to town finding new victims. His objective was a quick, one-time sale. He had little or no concern for the customers' financial welfare or needs. He was a one-man show; he was the focus of the sale. By the 1870s, his shady reputation had spread throughout the country, and his stereotype still remains.

In the early part of the 1900s, the approach to selling evolved from the individual entrepreneur to salesmen who were employed by companies. Still the image of the salesman did not improve very much. National companies found it necessary to develop sales forces. Since the individuals hired by the companies had varying degrees of competence in sales, companies standardized the approach to selling. The entrepreneurial "snake-oil" personality was not well suited to an employee status; therefore, as a way to ensure consistency in the quality and results of the presentations, a "canned" or "door-to-door" approach to selling was developed. Rather than relying on their individual inventiveness, salesmen were programmed to make a standardized sales pitch to any and all customers regardless of their situations or needs. The pitch was high pressure, and was geared at forcing a fast and often imprudent decision to buy. The *product* became the focus of the sale. The salesman basically memorized his "script" and made the same monologue presentation to all of his customers. Too often he misrepresented his products and continuously found it necessary to seek a new customer base because of attrition. His legacy to selling was the image of the high-pressure, slick salesman who would misrepresent the product, then "take the money and run."

The carryover of the snake-oil and door-to-door salesman is reflected in sales today in phrases such as "drum up business" and "foot in the door." Although not all solicitation salesmen of the 1800s and early 1900s were unscrupulous or high-pressure, the image of the flimflam man has lingered in the minds of many bankers.

SALES ROLE OF BANKERS

With sales having such a shady background, it is understandable that some bankers react negatively to selling as a primary part of their jobs. Bankers who resist their sales role view sales from its worst perspective, as selling people what they do not want, really cannot use, and cannot afford, rather than examining the ways in which selling can be mutually beneficial to the customer and the seller. Numerous bank studies clearly show that customers expect bankers to consult with them on the financial alternatives available to them, to improve their situations, to bring them new ideas, and to satisfy their needs. The emphasis on cash management and investment products is an example of the kind of sophisticated service customers demand from bankers. The kind of selling that is demanded in banking is not the selling of the past. Today's bankers are required to be consultants, advisers, and advocates of their customers and salespeople for their banks if they are to succeed. The objective of consultative selling is the development of long-term, mutually beneficial relationships, not one-time sales. Consultative selling is selling without misrepresentation or high pressure. Consultative selling is distinguished from other types of selling in its focus on the *customer's needs* rather than on the salesperson or the product. It is distinguished from high-pressure and door-to-door selling in the development of a sales dialogue rather than a monologue, and in the followup and nurturing that each account is given. There can be no "take the money and run" among bankers, since bankers must be concerned about customers' financial well-being, and the last thing they want is for customers to overextend themselves. The objective of the consultative sale is to conclude deals that are mutually beneficial and mutually profitable, so that long-term relationships can be developed.

Bankers who have resisted selling should work toward redefining what selling means to them. If the quintessential salesperson in their view is a flimflam man, they are missing the consultative aspect of sales in which the customer's needs and the bank's resources to satisfy those needs complement one another. If selling connotes to bankers manipulating someone to buy what he or she doesn't want or need, they understandably should want no part of it. Consultative sales aims at providing customers with what they need and indeed are demanding from banks or banking alternatives.

By selling or cross-selling, bankers are carving out a piece of the market while at the same time improving the customer's situation. By communicating effectively, bankers assist customers in making decisions with well-deserved confidence. Sales in banking is ethical, professional, and necessary for the customer and the bank. Sales results show on the bottom line, of course, but it is not a one-day tally that is the objective of sales in banking, but rather the long-term relationship.

Although there are many other effective approaches to sales, consultative selling provides bankers with a unique advantage: a framework that they can build on that can be consistently effective with a wide range of customers. It recognizes the special demands inherent in the banking industry: the wide range of credit and noncredit services, the wide range of customers and industries, and the highly competitive environment. It offers a flexible, fluid system of selling that can be applied by individual bankers to understand, control, and maximize their selling opportunities. Rather than develop a monologue presentation and monopolize the discussion, consultative bankers engage in a dialogue. They encourage customer input and guide that input through their selling skills.

Today's customers are sophisticated, and competitors in the banking industry are aggressive. Bankers who apply consultative strategies, in a marketplace in which product knowledge, communication skills, and follow-up skills are at best inconsistently practiced, have an edge over their competitors.

To consult effectively with their customers, bankers must have:

Up-to-date, sales-oriented product knowledge

Understanding of the needs of their customers

Consultative selling skills

Strategies for developing and managing accounts

Ongoing training support and reinforcement from managers

If any of these sales tools are missing, sales effectiveness is significantly reduced. Bankers who have these resources have the opportunity to succeed in today's marketplace.

2
Product Knowledge

PRODUCT KNOWLEDGE AS THE FOUNDATION OF SELLING

In order to maximize sales opportunities, bankers must have knowledge of a wide range of noncredit, credit-related, and credit products or services that their bank offers. Noncredit and credit-related products can and must be used to expand, solidify, enhance, and safeguard banking relationships. These services provide a way to open doors with prospects whose present bankers are not as aggressive, prepared, or aware as they might wish, and to close doors on competitors by establishing a total banking relationship that satisfies the spectrum of customer needs.

During the sales interview, bankers should mentally scan for selling or cross-selling opportunities. In their sales role, unless they have had a specific referral or inquiry from a customer or prospect, bankers cannot effectively approach a selling opportunity with only one product in mind. Particularly on prospect calls, bankers should probe for needs as well as an understanding of the customer's business *before* initiating a discussion of a specific product. Bankers who go in prepared to discuss only one preselected product may find the interview terminated all too quickly because they do not strike a responsive chord. Bankers require an understanding of a *range of products* so that they can tap the appropriate product from their reservoir of product information, as they recognize and maximize opportunities.

Doing homework prior to making a call is a first step in identifying customer needs. For example, in reading a balance sheet or a company's annual reports, bankers may identify opportunities for investment instruments such as Certificates of Deposit, Master Notes, Commercial Paper, and so on. Or in learning that the professional staff of a company travels a great deal, bankers can identify an opportunity for marketing Direct Deposit of Payroll. After making assumptions concerning customer needs, bankers must be prepared with need-evoking, probing questions in order to test or confirm these assumptions and to ensure that their product discussions are relevant to the customer's needs and interest.

Unless they have a general knowledge of the products important in their market area, bankers will be unable to recognize and respond to opportunities directly or indirectly signaled by customers. Without a knowledge of the bank's range of products and capabilities, bankers will not be in a position to switch gears when new needs are revealed, or to maximize opportunities they have already recognized.

Understanding the range of products offered by their bank is often a difficult and time-consuming task for bankers. Banks throughout the country offer from 20 to 200 products to their corporate, international, retail, and personal trust customers. Bankers are not required to understand all of the products marketed by the bank, but they must be familiar with the ten or 20 credit and noncredit products that are relevant to their specific market area. For example, market studies indicate that bankers are expected to know their bank's credit and noncredit capabilities (cash management, money market, and international) if they are to secure loan business and be of value to their customers. In addition, Bankers are being asked to *initiate* business and to cross-sell, since the strength of the banking relationship is dependent on developing a multiservice relationship.

What are the alternatives to providing bankers with useful, up-to-date product knowledge information? Unfortunately, without adequate product information the alternatives are *lost opportunities* and *lost market share*. Without product information bankers are often reluctant to initiate cross-selling calls, and those who do take the initiative find it difficult to capitalize on opportunities and are not eager to try again.

Interviews with more than 1000 bankers reveal an extreme need for product knowledge. Thus it may be helpful to examine the kind of product knowledge that bankers should have during prospecting, selling, and cross-selling sales calls, and to consider a bankwide system that could provide bankers with up-to-date, sales-oriented product information on an ongoing basis.

SALES-ORIENTED PRODUCT KNOWLEDGE

Product knowledge is the foundation of sales. There are different kinds of product knowledge: technical, developmental, generic, promotional, and sales oriented. Although all kinds of product information are important, not all are appropriate for bankers with cross-selling responsibilities. Too often bankers are given technical or promotional product information. Since bankers are often responsible for cross-selling as many as ten or 20 or more products marketed in their area, it is inappropriate and impossible to give them the degree or kind of technical information that product specialists have. The kind of product information contained in a brochure designed for the customer is not suitable, either, since it merely puts the banker on an equal footing with the customer and usually does not provide sufficient information for *initiating* a sale or *recognizing* a cross-selling opportunity. Bankers should have more information about products than their customers but less than the specialists. Bankers who call on customers need up-to-date, sales-oriented product information most, but they are often the last to receive it.

RESOURCES FOR PRODUCT KNOWLEDGE

It may be helpful to examine how bankers develop their product knowledge and what resources are available to them. Bankers have individual access to product specialists; they can attend seminars or product workshops; they can discuss products with their managers; they can go on "tandem" or "joint" calls with more experienced officers or specialists. They can gain product knowledge from banking literature or from banking associations, from advertisements by their bank or competitive banks. They can be coached by their managers and learn from their customers. They can and do learn a great deal through their own experiences. All of these resources are valuable, but they are time consuming and not always readily available. An additional resource for bankers is the traditional service catalogue. But although bankers have immediate access to it, the information and the catalogues themselves are usually fraught with problems.

Problems with Traditional Service Catalogues

The most obvious problems are size and accuracy. Because they are frequently cumbersome and inconvenient to carry or use, they are relegated to a shelf. And because they are so time-consuming to compile, they frequently get out of date even before distribution and tend to remain that way.

Just as important as the size and accuracy problems is the *kind* of information presented in the service catalogue. Too often such catalogues are technical manuals that provide little or no information relevant to a selling situation. The two or three pages dedicated to each product tend to be "get-acquainted" pieces rather than viable sales tools.

Another problem with service catalogues and indeed most product knowledge resources is that they are often treated in an isolated manner rather than as a system that is tied to an overall marketing plan and implemented as a part of sales, sales management, or relationship training.

For these reasons the traditional service catalogue does not meet the crying need bankers have for the kind of product knowledge that is called for during a sales call. The traditional service catalogue, although at one time a satisfactory resource, does not provide today's bankers with the kind of product information required to carry out successfully the *new responsibilities* of initiating business or selling noncredit and credit-related products that are a part of the competitive and aggressive banking industry.

Bankers should be provided with an alternative to the service catalogue to supplement the development of their product knowledge. They should request that the responsible unit (marketing, a specific division, product management, training, personnel) provide up-to-date, sales-oriented product information on the key products marketed by the bank. Bankers, because of time factors, should not have to develop their own product knowledge resources. The persons responsible for disseminating product information should work with those in the bank who have the most experience and expertise with the products from an operational and sales point of view. Product information should be conveniently available to all bankers with sales responsibilities, since product knowledge provides the very basis of selling.

An Alternative to the Service Catalogue

As an alternative to the service-catalogue, banks can profile each product *individually*. Rather than placing all of the bank's products in one large catalogue or several divisional catalogues, the profiling approach breaks the product knowledge down into smaller, more manageable units, with one product per unit. A folder-sized, individual profile on each product is a viable alternative for developing and disseminating product information, since the profiles immediately solve the size problems by offering a convenient, lightweight alternative. The individual folders also solve the content problem because they have the room and perspective to provide more than internal technical details of the products. The content of each profile should provide bankers with what they need to initiate sales calls and conduct effective sales interviews.

Each profile should be product specific. For example, in the cash management area, there could be a possibility of five to ten individual profiles, such as:

Account Reconcilement

Automated Balance Reporting

Depository Transfer Checks

Direct Deposit of Payroll

Lock Box

Zero-Balance Accounts

Other cash management products

Each product for which there is a market focus should be profiled. A bank can have as few as ten profiles or as many as 200. Many money-centers and regional banks profile between 20 and 30 key products. (See list below.)

The objective of each profile is to assist bankers in recognizing and maximizing cross-selling opportunities. The profiles should be indexed and cross-referenced by industry and product group to facilitate cross selling. Of course, the content of the profile is critical. It should be more comprehensive than the material usually contained in a service catalogue. Too little information is ineffectual; too much information defeats its own purpose. Bankers require a *basic body* of information on every product for which they have selling and cross-selling responsibilities, and this basic information should be readily available to them. The following 23 critical categories should be available to bankers for all products for which they have marketing responsibilities.

TWENTY-TWO CRITICAL PRODUCT KNOWLEDGE CATEGORIES FOR A SALES INTERVIEW

Seminars, interviews, and field experience with more than five thousand bankers from regional and money-center banks have identified the kinds of specific product information that are likely to be needed during sales calls. The following categories represent the 22 as aspects of a product that bankers generally need to know:

Fundamental description of the product

Customer needs

Features linked with benefits

Qualifying criteria and target market

Decision-making unit

Representative customers

Probing questions

Objection and responses

Competitive standing

Case history

Action step

Product implementation

Product operations

Pricing and pricing rationale

Product information checklist

In-bank contact for further information

Start-up time

Documentation

Cross-sell alert

Product family

Exhibits

Feedback summary

Bankers require information pertaining to the 22 categories on their range of key products if they are to be alert and responsive to customer signals and sales opportunities. Customers continually reveal needs and problems, but unless bankers understand the capabilities of the bank, they will fail to recognize opportunities and maximize them. Following is a review of what information should be contained in each of the 22 categories.

Description

Each profile should begin with a general overview of the product that gives a fundamental description of the generic aspects of the product and of the unique aspects of the bank's product. It should explain what the product is, what it does, how it basically works, who the target audience is, how it could possibly benefit a customer, and how it fits into the bank's marketing plan.

Features and Benefits

Features are the *qualities* or characteristics that the bank puts into the product; benefits are the values derived by the customer. Features and benefits are the heart of sales-oriented product knowledge. There is no better way to understand a product than by understanding its features and benefits, and there is no better way to sell a product than by linking its features to its benefits. Features and benefits help bankers link the technical aspects of the product with the customer's needs. They help bankers understand the product from the *customer's point of view.* Understanding and linking features and benefits enable bankers to look at a product from a sales perspective rather than from the technical or operational viewpoint. (See pages 65–68 for a discussion of features and benefits.)

Qualifying Criteria

An important factor in prospecting is recognizing the qualifying criteria for the product. Qualifying criteria are the characteristics that make a customer eligible for a product. Without knowing the qualifying criteria for products, bankers may miss sales opportunities or waste time discussing products that are not appropriate for a customer.

To determine whether a customer qualifies for a product, bankers should have the following product information:

1 General criteria (target market)
2 Specific criteria that render the customer eligible:
   • Volume
   • Dollar
   • Legal or geographic limitations
   • Credit implications
   • Relationship with the bank

- Target market
- Industry focus

For example, one of the *general criteria* for Import Letter of Credit service is that the customer be an "importer of raw materials, equipment, or finished goods that qualifies for a line of credit or specific approval supported by cash." *Specific criteria* for a particular bank would include "an average letter of credit of not less than *$7000 per issuance* and *minimum of monthly usage* of the Letter of Credit," as well as "an account with the bank."

It is very important that bankers understand the basis for any particular qualifying criterion. Although many banks' products are flexible and can be tailored to meet customer requirements, bankers should not exceed options provided by the bank unless the special requirements are warranted and approved. Customers frequently will ask for all kinds of special treatment or "bells and whistles." Bankers should find out what the customer hopes to achieve by these special requests. By applying their product knowledge, bankers can often demonstrate to the customer how a particular system that the bank uses will satisfy the stated desire.

For example, when cross-selling Lock Box services, bankers are often confronted by customers who prefer to keep their own lock box numbers instead of the new ones provided by the bank. On the surface, this seems very sensible. "Why can't you pick up from my box?" customers will ask. An informed banker would explain:

I can appreciate the work involved in organizing your internal collections systems. Naturally, you wouldn't want to modify this system unless there were substantial advantages to you. I would like to learn a little more about your system to determine whether if and how our Lock Box service might benefit you.

How often do you presently collect your remittances? I think that you will find that our Lock Box will help you there. We will pick up your mail eight times through a 24-hour period. Our Lock Box has a unique zip code that can accelerate the delivery of remittances by reducing mail float [the time it takes a payment to reach its destination] and thereby improve your cash flow. What are your thoughts on the advantages of using our unique zip code to accelerate your cash flow?

To qualify for Lock Box service, a customer is required to use the bank's number. By understanding the qualifying criteria and the reasons for them, bankers can cooperate with operations, and at the same time satisfy customer needs and concerns.

Sometimes bankers, in their enthusiasm to meet customer needs, agree to options that place unnecessary burdens on the operations and service area and may in fact reduce the quality of the service to the customer. This frequently results in internal difficulties for the operations area, dissatisfaction from the customer who does not receive what he or she thought had been purchased, and strained relations between operations and the line. By understanding the criteria and capabilities of a product, bankers can increase internal as well as external satisfaction.

In addition to creating a satisfactory relationship between customers and the bank, and between bankers and the operations area of the bank, attention to qualifying criteria is an important time-management, prospecting, and cross-selling tool. Spending time with false prospects is expensive and unproductive for both bankers and their customers. Understanding qualifying criteria can assist bankers in separating "suspects" from prospects and can thereby save and maximize time. Qualifying criteria can also help customer relations, since bankers who have inaccurate or incomplete qualifying criteria can convey a poor image for the bank or even damage a relationship by having to back out of a sale and decline after initiating the discussion. For example, a banker may interest a customer in Lock Box Service only to find out that he or she does not have the required number of mailed remittances. Qualifying criteria can also help bankers identify cross-selling opportunities with present customers, or enable them to substitute products when customers don't qualify for a particular product.

Qualifying criteria revolve around three critical considerations:

1 Is the customer eligible for a particular product?
2 Does the product satisfy the customer's needs?
3 Can the banker effect a mutually beneficial relationship between the customer and the bank?
4 Should the banker commit to the customer?

Qualifying criteria help bankers match the product with the customer. In determining whether the product and the customer complement one another, bankers should consider:

The specific qualifying criteria for the product
The eligibility of the customer
The customer's needs
The responsiveness of the product to the customer's needs
The decision maker's understanding of this need
Benefit to the customer
Profitability for the bank

Understanding the specific qualifying criteria of a product will enable bankers to identify prospects and initiate discussions.

Decision-Making Unit

To be more effective and to save time, bankers should direct their sales efforts to the decision maker or the decision influencer. They should have information concerning the appropriate position to be contacted for specific products. In discussing Foreign Exchange, bankers should set appointments with the treasurer, foreign exchange manager, or international cash manager, depending on the organization of the company. For Certificates of Deposit, bankers should probably see an investment officer, portfolio manager, treasurer, or individual investor. Although the treasurer seems to be a person to see for most bank products, it is important that the identity of key decision makers be known. In developing their contacts, bankers should remember to develop "depth contacts" by meeting with the high (economic) decision makers and the wide (user) decision makers. Establishing "high and wide" contacts helps ensure support and minimizes internal undermining in the company based on misinformation, fear, or politics. (See pages 125–128 for a discussion of the decision-making unit.)

Representative Customers

Although a specific individual's name may not be provided, bankers should be given the names of companies that are satisifed by the bank's service. It is appropriate to secure permission from these companies to list them as satisfied users. Some products, such as Personal Trust, because of their confidential nature, do not lend themselves to the listing of specific references.

Probing Questions

Bankers should be given specific, probing questions for each product to assist them in opening their product discussions, in qualifying a customer, and in uncovering needs. These questions should be open ended, requiring more than a yes or no reply. Probing questions are an excellent way to interest the customer in the sales interview, since they involve him or her in the sale. Probing questions are the questions that product specialists and other seasoned bankers, based on their years of experience, know to be effective in initiating and maintaining a sales dialogue. (See pages 54–57 for a discussion of probing questions.)

Objections and Responses

Although objections concerning a particular product or a particular bank may be new to the banker, they have probably been stated many times before. Bankers with or without sales experience in a particular product should, whenever possible, be prepared for inherent objections and should construct the basis of the responses *before* meeting with the customer. When bankers have anticipated the objections that experience demonstrates are likely to be raised, they are better prepared to stay in the sale, complete the sale, or make a qualified referral to the specialists. (See pages 68–94 for a complete discussion of objections.)

Competitive Information

To maximize sales opportunities, bankers should have information on their *competitors' products as well as their own*. Competitive information enables bankers to point out (and create) their own product advantages. An understanding of the competitors' products is the key to carving out a competitive edge among products that *appear* to be similar. Without competitive information, bankers cannot compare their competitors' strengths and weaknesses with their bank's competitive selling points. Because competitive information is not easily gathered, bankers can be susceptible to customer pressures about competitive offers or rumors or misperceptions about their own product's failings. The three key ingredients for selling are one's own product knowledge, competitive knowledge, and customer knowledge. Without competitive information bankers cannot answer objections concerning "other offers," nor can they appreciate their own bank's capabilities. Bankers should know who their major competitors are and also the "trade" names for the competitor's products.

Following is an example of competitive information:

Product: Check Reconcilement

Competition's Strengths	Competition's Weaknesses	Our Competitive Selling Points
	X Bank	
Volume over 500 items (Ours 1000 items.)	Uses purchased hardware, therefore is less flexible	Offers four different reports
Offers checks retention or check destruction	More errors	Personal service from account officer who stays involved as liaison
More branches	Higher price for options	Manual and automated
		Competitive item charge
		Prompt turnaround (complete reconcilement in seven days)
		Our own in-house system, which is more flexible
	Y Bank	
More branches	Small, inexperienced staff	Experienced staff
Flexible in-house system		Total cash management consulting capabilities

Although specific competitive information is very difficult to gather, bankers should have such information on all of their major competitors if they are to help customers compare price and value. Competitive information is a two-way exchange. It should be provided continually by the bank to the bankers and by the bankers to the bank; line bankers should report field developments to product or divisional management, who in turn should report technical and marketing developments to line bankers. (See Feedback Summary, page 27.) Of course, it is unprofessional to use competitive information in a derogatory way. Rather, competitive information should be used to help customers make objective comparisons.

Case History

Case histories are useful in supporting how customers benefited. They provide an example of the product in action. In presenting a case history, the banker should discuss the situation or problem that existed, the bank action that corrected the problem, and the customer benefits in terms of time savings, efficiency, accuracy, peace of mind, and dollars.

Action Step

Bankers should be familiar with the different action steps for products marketed in their area. The action step is the first step in implementing the product. It should be used to conclude the meeting and to *establish the next step* as a way to get the ball rolling. Action steps turn "hello calls" into sales calls. Action steps will vary according to the type and complexity of the product and the customer's situation, but they can range from setting an appointment with a specialist to completing the sale. For example:

> When would it be convenient for a cash management specialist to contact you to discuss a Lock Box study to determine the most efficient way to process your remittances?

Setting a specific action step and following up are the responsibility of the banker. Possible action steps should be planned *prior* to making the sales call and should be tied to the sales call objective. (See pages 99–101, Action Step.)

Implementation Process

Bankers should know the steps that *they,* the *customer,* and the *product specialist* must take to get the customer on board and to implement the product. Implementation steps include qualifying the prospect, gathering data, introducing the product specialist or the technical person, seeking and attaining internal approvals (if credit related), and arranging for and completing all operational testing procedures and document signing. For example, one step of the implementation process for Foreign Exchange Service would be: Calling officer makes recommendation to Credit Committee that an unconfirmed foreign exchange line be extended to the customer. The implementation process should clearly define who takes *what* steps and *when, where, how* and in *what order* each step occurs.

Operational Process

In relationship banking, the sale begins *after* the decision to buy is made. Bankers should be aware of the *follow-up* operational procedures and activities that take place during the life of the product after the customer has signed up. By understanding the operational procedures, bankers can assist the customer if there are problems and can respond to questions concerning service or delivery. For example, one step of the operating procedures for Letters of Credit would be: Letters of Credit Department notifies applicant if there are discrepancies in the documents and gives payment advices. . . .

Pricing

Pricing is a critical feature of any product. Bankers should be aware of not only the fees and balances for a particular product but also the fee parameter, and special situations that require input from the technical specialists to determine pricing. Bankers should remember that price is a product feature, and when discussing price they should treat it like any feature by linking it to its benefits. Pricing information is critical, and bankers should not be deprived of it simply because it is negotiable based on options or the total relationship. Bankers should be given pricing parameters, and instructions to defer price to specialists when the pricing requires input from them. Many banks are rethinking their pricing structure to determine the profitability of the noncredit and credit-related products. Management should conduct pricing studies, make pricing and marketing determinations, and provide bankers with pricing and marketing rationales.

For example, for Foreign Exchange, the following guidelines might be given:

Pricing. Market rates that change minute to minute. No additional charge. . . .

Profitability. Profit comes from spread between purchase and sale price.

Marketing Rationale. Enhances bank's image as full-service bank. Opportunity to cross-sell. . . . Strengthens relationship.

In-Bank Contact

Bankers should be given the names and extensions of in-bank specialists to be contacted for additional product information. Convenient access to specialists is essential if bankers are to make referrals or have their questions answered.

Start-up Time

Customers almost always want to know when they can begin using a product, and bankers should know how long it will take to get a product operational. Even if volume or complexity is a factor that affects start-up, bankers should be given the time parameters, since efficient and timely start-up can be a strong competitive selling point. One regional bank got substantial (and long-term) Import Letter of Credit business from a national company because it was able to approve the line and implement the service in one and a half days.

Documentation

Bankers should be familiar with the documents or contracts to be signed and the forms to be completed to ensure smooth implementation. They should be prepared to explain any complex or unique agreements, such as the loan agreement for Master Notes.

Cross-Sell Alert

Bankers should be aware of the relationship among the bank's products and use the sale of one product as a hinge to sell other related or sometimes unrelated products that satisfy the customer's needs or improve his or her situation. For example, a company that uses Import Letter of Credit may be an excellent candidate for Foreign Exchange, and a company that uses Account Reconcilement may be an excellent candidate for Balance Reporting.

Product Family

Often a particular product fits into a product area, and bankers should have an understanding of this. For example, Depository Transfer Checks is a product in the cash management area. This "product family" consists of:

Cash Management

Collections	Disbursements	Cash Reporting Control
Concentration Accounts	Account Reconcilement	Balance Reporting
Depository Transfer	Controlled Disbursements	
Checks	Money Transfers	
Lock Box	Payable through Drafts	
Wire Transfers	Zero-Balance Account	

Exhibits

It is helpful for bankers to have convenient access to brochures, sample letters, advertisements, or other materials relevant to the product. (See pages 128–131, Sales Materials.)

Feedback from the Line

The categories discussed so far represent information directed from the specialists or operations area to the line bankers. Just as management should see to it that product information is channeled on an ongoing basis to line bankers in the field, it should encourage the flow of communication from the line to the specialists. The specialists have a great deal of information about the bank's own products, and bankers who have day-to-day, face-to-face contact with customers frequently have a great deal of information about competitive products and market trends and demands. Because of their customer contact, they are often aware of market developments and competitive changes *before* specialists or management. When management does not tap this source of market information, it loses the opportunity to identify market trends, initiate product advancements, make pricing or product adjustments, and respond to new ideas.

Compiling data about key competitors is not simple, and since bankers are the ones who have bits and pieces from their customers, their information must be pooled if a clear competitive picture is to be developed. Open communication between line bankers and product specialists or operations is very important if market opportunities are to be seized.

All information from the line is of great importance in the marketing effort. Too often it is banker's own misperceptions about a product's "inferiority," not any superiority of the competition, that hurts the sale of the product. Such misperceptions should be corrected if market share is to be maintained. Bankers can communicate important competitive information in various ways, such as sales meetings and product seminars. Too often, however, vital information is lost over coffee or in a passing comment. Managers should encourage bankers to feed back in-the-field information (consistently and systematically). To facilitate centralizing competitive information, bankers should submit their feedback to their managers, and managers should forward the hard data or hearsay and all other information to the appropriate areas. By systematically channeling information into the bank and by verifying and sharing the researched information, bankers can not only multiply the benefits of their sales experience but can also contribute to product improvements.

A feedback form placed at the end of each individual profile, a category on a call report, or a feedback tablet for bankers can be an effective way to collect and monitor information from the line. The feedback should be used to relay the following kinds of information:

Competitive information (pricing, service, capabilities)
Product disadvantages and advantages (verified or perceived)
Objections

Exhibit 1　Sample Feedback Form

Name of Product: _____ Date: _____

Information on Competitors (pricing, service, capabilities, market thrust, market penetration, new customers, changes in product, marketing brochures)

_____
_____
_____
_____

Competitive Disadvantages and Advantages for Our Product (bankers' or customers' perceptions—rumors or hard data)

_____
_____
_____
_____

Additional Objections, Probing Questions, Benefits

_____
_____
_____
_____

Comments or Suggestions

_____
_____

Source of Information or Situation (optional)

_____

Signature: _____ Ext.: _____ Date: _____

Please Foward to: _____

_____

Additional customer benefits

Comments or suggestions

The feedback forms should be submitted to managers and responded to by product management or the department responsible for product or business development.

SALES LINE

The alternative to providing bankers with this kind of crucial sales information on their key products is their missing countless opportunities to strengthen relationships by selling and cross-selling. The following line represents a *sale:*

Initiate the sale

Implement the sale

Referral points to specialists

The categories of product information contained in a Product Profile are designed to help bankers *get on* and *stay on* the sales line. Using this information, bankers are expected to advance to a particular stage in the sale depending on the complexity of the product. At each point in the sale, bankers may make a referral to a specialist.

For those who think these categories may contain too much information, it is important to consider the objectives of disseminating product information. Bankers are being asked to *initiate* business. These categories will provide them with the kind of information they need to initiate sales calls confidently and to complete them successfully. Without adequate sales-oriented product information on a *range* of products, bankers will be unable to recognize or capitalize on the signals sent directly or indirectly by customers during a sales interview.

Developing this kind of product information may seem time-consuming, but in the long run it saves time. Unless bankers have five to ten years (as they did in the past) to become seasoned by going the rounds of the organization, they should have convenient access to up-to-date, sales-oriented product information on all products relevant to their market area as a way for them to accelerate their development, receive support in their sales activities, and keep abreast of the daily changes.

PRODUCT KNOWLEDGE QUESTIONS

Bankers with cross-selling responsibilities can make sure they have sufficient information on each product marketed in their area by considering the following questions *before* initiating cross-selling discussions with customers:

What is the product and how does it work?

How does the product tie into a customer's needs or situation?

What are the primary features and benefits of each product?

What are the qualifying criteria for customer eligibility?

Who are some customers who use this product?

Who is the decision maker?

What probing questions should be asked to uncover needs and qualifications and lead into the discussion to interest the customer?

What objections are likely to be raised? What are the main points to use in resolving the objections?

What action should be taken at the conclusion of the meeting as a firm next step?

Who is the primary competition in this area?

What is an appropriate case history?

What is the pricing structure?

Who is the specialist for the product or the in-bank contact for additional information?

How long does it take to get started once an agreement to use the product or service is reached?

What are the operational procedures (before and after signatures)?

What materials, brochures, and further data are available?

The following list illustrates the wide range of products that can be provided by banks.

Representative Product List:
Commercial Products

Acceptance Financing

Automated Payroll

Asset-Based Financing (Accountings Receivable Financing, Inventory, Equipment)

Account Reconciliation Plan

A Forfait Financing

Bank Safekeeping

Balance Reporting

Bankers Acceptances

Cash Letters (Domestic, International)

Credit Line

Custodian Service

Certificates of Deposit

Commercial Loans

Commercial Checking Accounts

Commercial Paper (Investment, Issuance, Agency)

Commercial Finance (Asset-Based Financing)

Corporate Bond Services (Registrar, Paying, Agent, Transfer Agent)

Corporate Stock Services

Corporate Savings Accounts

Corporate Trustee—Indenture

Corporate Finance Advisory

Coupon Collection/Cremation

Custody of Securities

Depository Transfer Checks

Direct Deposit Payroll (Automated Clearing House Payments)

Direct Lending

Divestitures

Documentary Drafts

Employee Benefit Plan (record keeping)

Employee Stock Option Plan Purchase and Dividend (ESOP)

Escrow Services

Equipment Finance

Eurobond Financing

Eurobond Purchase and Sale

Eurocurrency Syndicated Loans

Eurodollar Deposit

Executorship

Eximbank

Export Financing (Eximbank, Hermes, COFACE, etc.)

Factoring (Commercial Finance)

Federal Funds—Purchase and Sales

Foreign Accounts Receivable Financing

Foreign Collections—Inward and Outward

Foreign Exchange Advisory

Foreign Exchange Trading (Foreign Currency)

Foreign Remittances

Industrial Sales Finance (Vendor Financing)

International Cash Management Products

International Paying and Receiving

Investment Advisory

Investment Counseling

Investment Management

Letters of Credit

   Import

   Export

   Standby

   Documentary

   Reimbursement (banks)

Lock Box (Wholesale and Retail/Manual and Automated)

Leverage Leasing

Master Trust

Master Notes

Municipal Notes and Bonds

Payable through Drafts
Paying Agent for Municipal Bonds
Peer Trusts
Pension Plan Portfolio Management
Preauthorized Checks
Private Placement
Project Financing
Payroll Processing
Repurchase Agreements
Retirement Benefit Plans
Safekeeping (Depository Trust Company)
Securities Collections
Self-Employed Benefit Plans
Short-Term Tax Exempts
Tax Exempt Municipal Bonds
Testamentary Trusts
Term Loans (Secured, Unsecured)
Transfer Agent
True Lease
   International
   Leverage Investor
   Single Investor
Trustee under a Will
U.S. Dollar Clearing
U.S. Treasury Bills and Notes
Wire Transfers
Zero-Balance Accounts

Consumer Products

Auto Leasing
Auto Loan
Automated Teller Machine

Automated Transfer Service

Automobile Loans

Bank by Mail

Certificates of Deposit

Certified Checks

Checking Accounts

Collections

Coupon Collections

Direct Deposit of Payroll, Dividends, Social Security

Discount Brokerage

Foreign Currency or Foreign Exchange

High-Interest Savings

Holiday Club

Home Improvement Loans

Individual Retirement Accounts

Investment Management

Keogh Plans

Line of Credit—Personal

Liquid-Loophole Certificate

MasterCard

Merchant Banking

Money Market Instruments

Money Orders

Mortgages

NOW Accounts

Overdraft

Pay by Phone

Payroll Deduction

Personal Line of Credit

Personal Loan

Point of Sales

Preauthorized Payments

Regular Checking Account

Regular (Passbook) Savings

Savings Certificates

Safe Deposit Boxes

Safe Keeping

Statement Savings

Tax-Free Certificates

(All Savers)

Student Loans

Telephone Transfer

Travelers Checks

Trust Services

Utility Payments

U.S. Savings Bonds

Visa

TYING PRODUCT KNOWLEDGE TO CUSTOMER NEEDS

Customers make financial decisions every day. Bankers who understand their customers' objectives, constraints, problems, and priorities in tandem with their own bank's products or services can recommend alternatives, promote their banks' products, and satisfy customer needs.

Bankers cannot satisfy their customers' needs without understanding them. Since those needs are not always *immediately* visible, bankers must use research and the *sales interview itself* to identify and confirm needs. Developing customer knowledge is often time-consuming and difficult. The bank's market research department, a company's annual report, financial report resources, trades, other customers, and customers themselves can provide bankers with valuable customer information prior to the sales call. Developing customer information requires that bankers be resourceful: If up-to-date resources are not available, bankers should call company switchboards to confirm names and titles or ask for information concerning the organization. Sometimes important information can be gathered from a conversation with a switchboard operator or a secretary.

Bankers should gather as much data as possible about a customer *prior* to making sales calls.

Company Knowledge Questions

What is the company's business (wholesale, retail, manufacturer, etc.)?

What are its products? Which are most profitable?

Who is the chief financial officer

How centralized is the decision-making unit?

Who makes the decisions about cash management, trade services, and so on?

Who are the most appropriate contacts in the company?

Who are the key decision makers? Who are the influences (Bankers tend to call on senior management, but they often should also meet with operational personnel and introduce specialists from the bank to these company contacts.)

What are the social interests of the decision makers (entertainment/ correspondence)?

What are the names of the secretaries of the decision makers?

How long has the company been in business?

What is the size of the company (annual sales volume, number of employees, or net worth)?

Where is the company located (county, town, city, zip code)?

What is the type of organization (headquarters, subsidiary)?

How does it compare in the industry (reputation with trade, customers, competition)?

What is the customer's relationship with the bank?

What are the company's other banking relationships?

Who is the lead bank?

What are the customer's goals and objectives?

What are the customer's constraints?

What difficulties, concerns, or needs does the customer have?

Is there a third-party referral?

Who are the company's lawyers, auditors?

Who is on the board of directors?

Does senior management of the bank know any of the company's decision makers?

What is the company's management style?

Sales Interview Fact Finding

These are some of the key questions that should be answered and should become a part of the customer information file. Information that cannot be gathered in advance of the sales interview should be gathered during the sales call. While waiting to see their customers, bankers might read in-house literature, talk to support personnel, and observe the business environment and the business facility. More important, bankers *should use the sales interview* to discover facts, test assumptions, and identify customer needs. Bankers often do not ask enough questions. By querying them in a positive and consultative manner, bankers can learn important information about their customers. Early in the sales interview, bankers should find out how a customer is presently handling particular aspects of his or her business and how satisfactory the present system is. They should be prepared with specific back-up questions to determine areas in which the customer's present systems can be complemented or improved.

A word of caution should be added here: Remember to give some information to the customer before asking questions. A brief introduction, a brief summary of events leading to the meeting, a statement of general objective, and hint of a possible benefit all provide excellent leads into questions about the customer's needs and interests.

Testing Assumptions

Questions are also useful in testing the validity of the assumptions bankers usually have concerning the customer's needs and their sales topic. Making assumptions based on homework and the banker's own experience with a particular industry or customer is a necessary part of planning for the sales call. It is important, however, for bankers to remember that assumptions are merely educated guesses that must be tested, modified, or confirmed prior to or during the sales interview, before action is taken on them.

By testing assumptions with probing questions, bankers can proceed with greater confidence that they are addressing the needs and concerns of the customer. Bankers who take the time to develop assumptions in their sales planning stage and to test them before engaging in a product discussion are likely to hit on topics of interest and be in a position to key in on products or alternatives that are relevant to the customer.

SUMMARY

Product knowledge is the foundation of sales. Bankers should understand their products from a sales perspective, and they should link their product knowledge to their customers' needs. The more information bankers have about their products and their customers, the more likely they are to recognize and bring out needs, develop viable solutions, and meld the product with the customer.

3
Consultative Sales Approach

TEN ELEMENTS OF A SALES INTERVIEW

Observation and participation in sales situations indicate that certain elements consistently occur during successful sales interviews. By understanding the sales elements it is possible for bankers to conduct more successful sales interviews on a consistent basis.

Ten elements of a sale were identified in role play and in field experiences with more than 1000 bankers. By managing them during sales interviews, bankers can increase their effectiveness. The following ten elements are isolated into ten distinct categories for discussion purposes, but they are by no means independent of one another. These are not sequential skills but rather are parallel skills. Although this framework is logical and simple, its mastery requires practice and experience.

The ten elements that consistently occur during successful consultative sales are:

1. *Opening.*
   - Greetings and introduction.
   - Rapport-building (optional).
   - Summary.
   - Selling the interview (objective and possible benefit).
   - Bridge question.
2. *Customer Motivation Lever.* Identifying the customer's primary needs and concerns.
3. *Probing questions.* Using open-ended questions to qualify the customer or uncover needs.
4. *Constructive Listening.* Paying attention to and *using* what the customer says.
5. *Features and Benefits.* Linking features with customer benefits.
6. *Fielding Objections.* Anticipating and responding to objections.
7. *Incremental Close.* Testing for agreement and understanding throughout the sales interview.
8. *Action Step.* Initiating the first step of the implementation process.
9. *Body Signals.* Using nonverbal communication to support, supplement, or evaluate what is verbally communicated.

10. *Sales Environment.*   Observing the setting for the sale and its impact on the sale.

With the exception of the opening, customer's Motivation Lever, and action step, which should be kept in sequence, all of the other elements are interspersed throughout the sales call. The opening and action step are stationary for obvious reasons, and the Motivation Lever, although not as stationary, must be uncovered *before* a discussion of a specific product begins.

An effective sales interview is a fluid, dynamic encounter, rather than a series of programmed steps or a preset sequence. Bankers can face an objection or question immediately, for example, in the opening. Certainly they should respond to the customer, but awareness of the ten elements listed above allows them to regain their balance. They can then return to the opening after they have addressed the customer's immediate concern without rushing into the product discussion before the customer's needs are identified and understood by both the banker *and* the customer. In this way bankers can maintain control of the course of the sales interview. By understanding the selling process, bankers can avoid having customers control the sale by rushing them in and out of topics.

Although the time frame, mix, formality, or comprehensiveness of each of the ten elements may vary from product to product, customer to customer, industry to industry, banker to banker, or relationship to relationship, these elements should be a part of *every* sale. By understanding them, bankers can individualize their sales interviews and develop a professional style that is effective for them with a wide range of customers. Bankers should not try to function as chameleons. By understanding the shells and ideas that comprise the consultative selling framework, bankers can develop their individual selling styles, which they can use to identify and satisfy customer needs.

Bankers who understand their products from their customer's point of view, encourage customer input, and satisfy customer concerns and objections can be in control of the sales interview. Unfortunately, the word *control* often has a negative connotation. Control is essential during the sales interview—not overbearing, dominant, and inflexible control, but flexible control in which bankers adjust and direct the sales interview to the customer's needs. Bankers should assume the leadership role during the sales discussion if they expect to have a role in formulating buy decisions. They should not go through the sales interview like a cork at sea but rather should channel and guide the sales discussion.

By utilizing the ten elements, bankers can pace the presentation, delay discussing topics that are premature or are a separate issue, or *consciously* direct the conversation to respond to needs as they emerge. An understanding of the sales process reduces the number of occasions in which bankers ask themselves *after* the sales interview, "What went wrong?" It also helps them understand an repeat "what went right." Most important, knowledge of the sales framework allows bankers to *recover* during a negative sales interview and turn it around.

The ten elements are designed to help bankers conclude mutually beneficial relationships in situations in which their products are a viable alternative and are basically competitive in price and quality. The ten elements also assist bankers in selling superior products by ensuring that customers recognize and appreciate the products' superiority.

All bank products have their strengths and weaknesses. It is the banker's ability to differentiate his or her bank's own products and *communicate the value* of the product relative to customer *needs* that distinguishes products, bankers, and banks. *This is one of the primary ways in which product differentiation can be established and accepted by customers.* Today bankers are the product, because it is their presentation of products and services to customers that plays a significant role in the customer's decision to buy.

Each of the ten elements is designed to develop and maintain a dialogue between bankers and their customers. The following sections examine each of the ten elements and its application in selling situations.

Opening

The Importance of the Opening

In consultative banking the opening is more than the greeting; it is actually the overture of the sales call, in which bankers prepare the customer by focusing on what is in the sales interview for the customer rather than focusing on the product or the bank's objectives. Since the impact of the opening is much greater than the time it takes to open, it may be helpful to examine how to maximize the first few minutes of the sales call in establishing a consultative tone.

Parts of a Consultative Opening

By understanding the purpose and content of the opening, bankers can feel more confident initiating calls with new and old customers alike. There are five activities that should be a part of every opening.

Greeting and Introductions. Depending on the nature of the relationship, the formality and length of time dedicated to the greeting and the introduction will vary. The introduction includes name of banker, name of bank, presentation of business cards, and so on. Judgment should come into play in determining the content and formality of the introduction; however, with the new customer who does not offer his or her first name, bankers should consider addressing the customer formally: *Ms., Miss, or Mr.* This gives the customer the opportunity to suggest a first-name basis, which often is a signal of rapport. Also, with a prospective customer who may not be familiar with the bank or the banker, the location of the bank and a brief description of the bank, the banker's position, and the bank's commitment to the industry or market are appropriate. A note about this starting mark: Bankers must be *on time* for their appointments if they don't want to spend the interview recouping lost ground or making excuses. When they are delayed because of travel problems, they should telephone to advise the customer.

Rapport Building or Warm-up. *Rapport building* refers to discussion of topics that are not directly related to the objective of the sales call. Many bankers comment on items of personal interest such as a painting or trophy to break the ice. Some bankers utilize the location, the trip, or a sports team as a warm-up. It is usually advisable to keep rapport building brief and business related, for example, commenting on an attractive new facility or a civic award. This warm-up period is often easier and more successful with customers with whom rapport has been established and personal interests have been identified than with new customers on prospect calls. Rapport building with new customers can be more difficult, but the benefits derived from it can be very helpful in establishing a common ground with customers. Bankers must exercise judgment in deciding whether or not to build rapport and should take cultural and geographic customs into consideration. This is the *optional* part of the opening, which can be utilized by bankers as they deem appropriate.

However, the importance of this part of the opening should not be under-estimated.

Summary.   After the greeting, introduction, and optional rapport building, bankers should be prepared briefly to *summarize the events that led to the meeting*. The summary can recap a former meeting, or refer to the events that brought about the meeting such as a third-party referral, an article in the paper, a new shopping center, a new branch of the bank, a new product, a change in organizational structure (bank's or customer's), or the telephone call that led to the appointment. The summary should lead into the *most important* part of the opening, the *selling of the sales interviews* in which the objective and possible value of the meeting to the customer are set.

Selling the Idea of the Interview.   After the summary, bankers should make a general statement related to their objective telling the customer why they are there. In this way they can begin to set the agenda for the meeting. The objective can be specific, such as understanding how the customer is keeping track of funds to see whether there is a way better to maximize funds (Balance Reporting), or very general, such as beginning a dialogue with a prospective customer to determine whether the bank can complement its present service. In all situations, the sales objective should be positioned as a potential customer benefit and in most situations bankers should have a few products in the back of their minds that homework and experience say are likely to be of value to the customer. After bankers state their objective and potential benefit, they should check to determine whether the customer is in agreement with their ideas. The selling of the interview occurs when the banker can link his or her agenda and call objective to the possible benefits that are likely to accrue to the customer.

Selling the interview serves to motivate the customer to participate in the sales interview. Customers will be motivated to participate when they perceive:

An opportunity to improve their situation by increasing profits, improving operations through new technology, improving their image, solving problems, or satisfying personal agendas.

An opportunity to avoid risk or loss.

Dissatisfaction with their current situation.

An opportunity to learn new information or ideas.

Unless customers perceive the possibility of one or more of these situations fairly early in the sales interview, they will not have the incentive to participate actively.

Bankers who sell the idea of the interview help the customer recognize the possible benefits that can accrue from the discussion. Of course, the benefits often must be general, to allow for flexibility in the sales interview. Selling the idea of the interview is accomplished by discussing the *possible* benefits that the customer may derive from a particular product or service. Bankers should avoid sweeping claims or overstatements during the opening to keep expectations at a realistic level and to establish credibility.

Bankers who sell the interview before selling a product are able to generate customer interest and involvement in the interview. Bankers who do not take the time to sell the idea of the interview by linking their objective with potential value to the customer may never succeed in getting the sales interview off the ground. They may find themselves midway through the call still looking for a topic or product that will spark customer interest. After selling the idea of the interview, bankers use a bridge question to enter into the Motivation Lever segment of the sale.

Bridge Question. Bankers bridge from the opening to the Motivation Lever segment of the sales interview by asking a question that is designed to *encourage the customer to talk about his or her situation.* The question or questions should be based on the banker's research or experience with the customer, the industry, the product, or the bank's capabilities. Bankers should prepare their primary questions as well as some backup questions to use with less responsive customers to encourage their input. They earn the right to ask questions about the customer's situation, systems, or present operating mode through the opening. The bridge question leads into the second element of the sale, the Motivation Lever.

The following is an example of a consultative opening leading to a bridge question.

Banker.	Good morning, Mr. Wilson. I'm Tom Alster with X Bank in Philadelphia. (Rapport building for several minutes about the new facility and neighboring construction). I am with the National Division, and our bank has a strong commitment to. . . . I appreciated the opportunity to speak with you on Tuesday and your taking the time to meet with me today.	Greeting and introduction
		Summary
	As we discussed, X Bank has developed a flexible cash management system that is being used by a number of companies in your industry, which may be of value to you in. . . . How does that sound?	Objective
		Checking for agreement
	Before going into details about our capabilities, it would be helpful if you could tell me a little about the movement of cash in your company. How are you currently collecting your remittance?	Bridge question
	How satisfied are you with the availability of . . . ?	Backup questions
	How do you fund your dispersement accounts?	
	How do you get your balance information?	
Customer.	As we handle it now. . . .	

The five opening activities—greeting and introduction, rapport-building, summary, selling the interview, and the bridge question—provide bankers with an organized and individual way to open the sales call. Although bankers' words, style, and mannerisms must be their own and vary according to the situation, the structure of the opening should remain the same. Although the content should vary, the process should not. The result is not a canned opening as in programmed or door-to-door selling, but rather a professional opening based on preparation. The objective of the five parts of the opening is to increase bankers' confidence and effectiveness in initiating business, and to help them to open in a consistently positive manner by giving them a way to organize their thoughts. The structure is polite, constructive, consultative, and realistic. As it is for other professionals, when bankers have an awareness of the process and have a plan for openings, they can exercise greater control over what takes place.

On prospecting calls, bankers are required to spend more on the introduction and the selling of the interview. In subsequent meetings the focus shifts to summarizing the last meeting and checking with the customer on the status of conditions, interests, problems, developments or a new product the customer has been using since the last meeting.

By understanding the opening process, bankers can confidently and professionally initiate the sales interview. Even with customers who begin to complain or object immediately after the greeting, bankers are better able to retain control. Bankers can listen to the customer's point of view, explanation, or problems, respond to what the customer has said, and *then go back to the part of the opening that was interrupted*. This sharp focus enables bankers to exercise control early in the sales interview and therefore exercise greater control over the sales results.

Strategies for Opening

The following strategies can be used by bankers to strengthen their openings during the summary or selling of the interview stage.

The Customer Benefit Strategy. A suggestion of a possible benefit should be a part of *every* opening. By suggesting the possibility of greater profits, improved service, or avoidance of a loss, bankers can gain the customer's attention. The *benefit strategy* requires that bankers know something about the customer's business, situation, and needs. For instance, a customer who owns a large gift shop and uses numerous Letters of Credit may be interested in consolidating them, reducing costs, and simplifying internal clerical in-house procedures. The benefits should be presented as *possibilities* that will be determined by the customer's situation and needs. Benefit openings should be low-key selling in which the words *may* and *possibly* are used to replace the exaggerated claims or sweeping statements that can make customers doubt bankers' credibility and cause them to retreat. A customer benefit opening transforms "I would like to discuss our Import Letter of Credit service" to "I'd like to discuss the ways in which we may be able to improve your turnaround time." Benefit opening strategy shifts the focus of the opening from the bank's capabilities to the customer's needs and situation.

Professional Compliment Strategy.   By doing their homework, bankers can utilize the compliment strategy to demonstrate interest and appreciation of the customer and his or her business. Professional compliments should be sincere, accurate, timely, and individualized if they are to be meaningful. An example of a professional compliment opening would be a reference to a new acquisition or an industry award.

Third-Party Strategy.   Having a third-party referral is perhaps the most positive way to begin an interview with a prospective customer. Bankers who are introduced or referred by a third party have a substantial advantage. They can make use of these referrals to get in the door; once there, they should establish a rapport and when necessary utilize their first contact to gain an introduction or access to other decision influencers or to the appropriate decision maker.

Hinge Strategy.   By using any mutual point of reference to create a connection with the customer, bankers can help establish common ground. A *hinge* can be anything from a letter sent by the banker or an article in the paper to a mutual acquaintance.

Customer or Industry Experience Strategy.   This strategy is a kind of professional name-dropping. By referring to a respected company that is similar in size and type of business or providing industry information, bankers can earn the customer's attention and demonstrate that they have a working knowledge of the customer's business. This strategy is particularly useful in meeting with customers who are not familiar with the bank or a particular product. When using specific company names, bankers should first secure permission. Bankers should take care to use the names to build confidence, not to imply ''me-tooism.''

The Question Strategy.   The bridge question should be a part of every opening. Initial questioning should be handled gently, rather than in the style of a prosecuting attorney. After bankers have given some information (greeting and introduction, rapport building, summary, and selling the idea of the interview), they should ask permission to ask some questions better to understand the customer's situation. These questions are most important in understanding the customer's point of view and frame of reference. It is important for bankers to use their questions to involve the customer and find out what is on his or her mind so that they can address relevant topics.

An example of a consultative opening utilizing a third-party referral, a benefit, and a bridge question is:

> Mr. Jones, I'm Tom Smith, X Bank. I appreciated the opportunity to speak with you last week. My discussion with John Williams, at your headquarters, indicated that you may be interested in looking at some alternative ways to collect your remittances to improve your cash flow, and he suggested I contact you. Have you had an opportunity to speak with him about . . . ? *Before we discuss how an alternative method may assist you in paying down your loans, it would be helpful if you could describe what concerns you. Have you . . . . ?*

Highly successful salespeople use the bridge question as the key to the entire sale.

Opening with Multiple Customers

Immediately following a sales interview, bankers are often introduced to other individuals in the same company. Whether the second meeting is with a corporate treasurer, a partner, or a family member, bankers should remember to reopen with each new contact. If bankers assume that their first opening will *automatically transfer* to the next person, they may find themselves discussing matters that threaten, overwhelm, confuse, or bore the customer. Regardless of how many individuals they meet, they should repeat, even if in a capsulized form, the introduction, summary, selling of the idea of the interview and bridge question before they begin a product discussion. Summarizing the initial meeting and checking for agreement are essential during miniopenings. Too many "in-the-bag" sales are lost because of a failure to reopen with new decision makers! Also if *during* the sales interview a new party joins the meeting, bankers should remember to recap and be alert for new needs.

Tone

The tone of the opening will influence the entire sales interview. It should be positive, clear, and genuine. Confidence should be conveyed by bankers during the opening. Confidence is an abstract quality; bankers' ability to demonstrate it is directly related to their preparation, experience, and familiarity with the opening process. The steps of consultative opening are not designed to substitute for individual style and experience but rather to accelerate developing a style that is effective, professional, and individual.

Summary

Preparation is essential if bankers are to be effective. They should utilize the opening to earn the attention and interest of the customer. During the opening, the sales environment is established. Preparation includes a planned format for the opening process and the content. The greeting and introduction, summary, rapport building, selling of the interview, and bridge question provide the framework that bankers can use to introduce their ideas effectively and confidently and earn the right to uncover the customer's Motivation Lever.

Motivation Lever

The Key to the Sale

The objective of the Motivation Lever is to identify and understand the customer's needs. *It is the key to the sale,* the most important part of every sales interview, since it is the part in which bankers gain insight into the customer's needs and point of view. During the Motivation Lever the customer is encouraged by questions to reveal his or her needs, interests, or situation.

There are two questions that are pivotal to uncovering the customer's Motivation Lever. The first has to do with the customer's *present situation* or method of doing something; the second aims at *clarifying the degree of satisfaction* (strengths and weaknesses) with the customer's present system versus optimal system or future plans. With answers to these questions, bankers can identify gaps and use further questions and product knowledge to highlight alternatives or opportunities. Unless bankers can uncover the customer's Motivation Lever, they can only guess at how best to use their sales time to interest customers and solve their problems or improve their situations.

Just as bankers are responsible for talking in the opening, the customer should be encouraged to express his or her ideas and needs during the Motivation Lever segment of the sale. The Motivation Lever is uncovered when the *customer talks* about his or her business, problems, concerns, situation, current banking relationships, or methods of financial management. After opening, bankers are in an excellent position to ask the customer if they may ask some questions to determine the possible value or advantages they might add. These bridge questions encourage a customer to express his or her thoughts about his or her company and particular banking needs or related needs.

The questions should be more worthy of bankers and the customer than the old standby, "How's business?" Unless the customer's situation is understood, bankers cannot consult effectively. If, for example, bankers think there may be a need or opportunity for Direct Deposit of Payroll, they would say, "Before discussing some ways that we might increase efficiency and reduce costs in your payroll operations, I need to know about your current system. How are you currently doing your payroll?"

The information revealed during the Motivation Lever provides the basis of the sales dialogue that will follow. By identifying a customer's Motivation Lever *before* discussing a product, bankers can eliminate having to run through a list of products, or of the features and benefits of a particular product, trying to hit on something that interests the customer. The Motivation Lever concept keeps the horse before the cart; it enables bankers to identify needs and concerns first and then to suggest products or solutions. By understanding the customer's Motivation Lever, bankers can also assist the customer in *identifying* and solving his or her problems.

The Motivation Lever is the hub of the consultative sales approach. It is the element that differentiates consultative selling from high-pressure or door-to-door selling. It is also the segment that, as experience with several thousand calling officers shows, is the most difficult to master. Finding a customer's Motivation Lever requires questioning, observing, listening, and integrating skills. It also requires patience and self-control. It means asking questions and listening for five, ten, 15, or more minutes to the customer's reply, and picking up *all of the key concerns* expressed by the customer, then referring to and using the information throughout the sales call.

The Motivation Lever part of the sale is initiated by a bridge question in the opening, which places the ball in the customer's court. Bankers are often reluctant to do this because they fear losing control. Control, however, is achieved by directing the sales interview, not monopolizing it. The Motivation Lever segment helps bankers to understand the customer's orientation and to focus on relevant products and relevant benefits. *Customers buy benefits, not features,* and the Motivation Lever reveals the specific benefits that will be of value to the customer. For example: the fact (feature) that the Stock Transfer System provides a printout in 24 hours may be of no concern to a customer who is having shareholder problems because of complaints about inaccuracies in names, amounts, and so on. But the fact that the bank's stock transfer system is completely on line and verified by a clerk, which results in virtually 100% accuracy, is a benefit that will be of value to the customer. The customer's Motivation Lever in this situation is to reduce shareholder complaints. Bankers who can identify problems are in a good position to solve problems and increase market share. Questions that are asked *early* in the sales interview are the key to unearthing needs and maximizing opportunities.

The best way to develop customer interest is to have the customer talk about his or her plans, problems, needs, and goals. This applies to customers and prospective customers alike. In many ways it may be easier to ask Motivation Lever questions of prospective customers since bankers are not expected to have a storehouse of information on them. It is equally important and perhaps more difficult to remember to probe with an "old" customer whom bankers know very well. One key way to keep a spark in a relationship and keep competitors away is to seek needs with present customers. For example, with a customer with a seven-year relationship with the bank, the banker could say, "We haven't talked in some time about reducing your interest bill. Let's spend a few minutes discussing . . . pick-up float. . . ." Unless a customer is given the opportunity to talk about his or her situation, bankers will not be in a position to create win-win situations.

Bankers cannot relate their products to customer needs unless the needs are visible and these needs must be recognized and acknowledged by bankers *and* customers alike. Too often bankers perceive needs and then attempt to sell without establishing with the customer that the need or benefit exists and is important to the customer. Although some customers are keenly aware of what they want or need, many are not aware of possible savings in time, money, opportunities, or more efficient systems.

Bankers should be prepared to help customers recognize needs and opportunities, giving ample time during the sales interview to the identification of the Motivation Lever.

Summary

The Motivation Lever is the central point of consultative selling, and all other elements of the sale revolve around it.

Action-step	Opening
Sales environment	Probing questions
	Motivation Lever
Incremental close	Constructive listening
Body signals	Features/benefits
	Objections/responses

The purpose of the other nine elements is to develop and satisfy the Motivation Lever. The Motivation Lever makes the other elements work by ensuring that they are relevant to the customer's situation. Identifying the Motivation Lever enables bankers to individualize their sales calls, to meet the diversified needs of customers, and to consult with their customers in a professional, competent, and action-oriented manner. When the Motivation Lever is identified, meaningful dialogues ensue.

The Motivation Lever is discovered through customer input; and customer input is primarily evoked through probing questions. Most customers will respond to relevant consultative questions. However, bankers should be prepared with backup questions for less responsive customers. After asking questions, bankers should be prepared to listen to their customers' replies and use what they hear to connect their customers' ideas and perceptions with their bank's products, services, and capabilities.

Probing Questions

Defining Probing Questions

One of the most important functions of probing questions during a consultative sales interview is to identify the customer's Motivation Lever. Probing questions enable bankers to identify the customer's needs and interests. They play an important role in developing a consultative sales interview, since probing questions are the primary tool for developing a dialogue.

Probing questions are open-ended questions that require more than a yes or no reply from the customer. Close-ended questions (questions that elicit a yes or no response) should be limited, since they provide little or no information about the customer's needs, motivations, plans, or thoughts and give bankers at best a so–so (yes–no) chance of pursuing a particular topic further. By using questions that begin with *what, when, where, how, why, to what extent,* and so on, bankers create dialogues and gain valuable insight and information into their customers' thinking. Valuable questions can also begin with phrases such as "How are you presently . . . ?" "How satisfied are you with . . . ?" "What are your thoughts on . . . ?" "What effect would . . . have . . . ?" "What specifically . . . ?" "What alternatives are you considering?" "What is included in their offer?" "When are you planning . . . ?" or "Who currently . . . ?" Such questions give the customer an opportunity to participate in an exchange of ideas and give bankers information they can use to formulate and develop their product discussion relevant to the customer's situation, needs, and interests.

Probing questions constitute a pivotal part of the consultative sales approach. Early in the sales interview they provide consultative bankers with a way to identify the customer's Motivation Lever and to create customer involvement. Probing questions also enable bankers to clarify objections and to test for agreement and understanding.

Unfortunately, probing questions are perhaps the most underutilized selling tool that bankers have. Without using probing questions, bankers run the risk of making long, drawn-out presentations that do not necessarily address the customer's needs or spark the interest of the customer.

Probing Questions during the Sales Call

Probing questions are the sales tools that convert the one-sided sales *presentation* to a *sales interview* in which there is an exchange of ideas. Probing questions create a sales dialogue. They should be planned prior to the sales call and can be used to:

1 Establish the customer's willingness to give input and to assist bankers in finding the customer's Motivation Lever: "First, I'd like to ask some questions, if I may. How are you presently handling your payroll?" (Payroll Service, Direct Deposit of Payroll)

2 Find out about the customer's present situation or attitudes: "What thoughts have you given to . . . ?" or "How satisfied are you with your current ability to maximize overnight investments or pay down your loan?" (Balance Reporting)

3 Assist a customer in recognizing and accepting the existence of a problem or an unsatisfactory situation: "What has been your experience with late deliveries?" (Import Letter of Credit)

4 Identify specific competitors or preferences: "To whom else have you spoken?" (Interest Rate Swaps)

5 Narrow down a general statement or vague objection such as "My account analysis is *always* late!": "When was the last time we were late, so I can look into this and find out what seems to be the problem?"

6 Discuss and compare Total Offers: "What do they require so we can compare value and pricing?" (Loan)

7 Probe for qualifying criteria: "How many checks do you issue per month?" (Account Reconcilement)

8 Clarify objections: "In what way is your payroll complicated?" or "How specifically do you think you may lose control of your accounts receivable?" (Direct Deposit and Lock Box)

9 Test for understanding or agreement: "How helpful will it be for you to receive your domestic balance information by 9:00 A.M., in time to make investment decisions?" (Balance Reporting)

10 Create a problem-solving collaborative environment by *prefacing* questions with a brief explanation and invitation to answer: "So that I can focus on . . . , what specific . . . ?"

Probing questions are multipurpose, since they enable bankers to:

1 Qualify a customer (qualifying criteria).
2 Create customer input and participation (consultative dialogue).
3 Identify customer needs, problems, and satisfactions.
4 Gauge the degree of customer understanding and agreement (incremental close).
5 Create customer awareness by assisting customers in selling themselves by reaching their own conclusions.
6 Modify their discussion to address customer concerns or perspective (flexibility and shifting of gears to address the customer's needs).
7 Determine priority products or features and benefits to be emphasized (key features and benefits of interest to the customer).
8 Increase their control of the sales interview (by using a question to return to a topic).

Probing Question Traps

Bankers reduce the effectiveness of their probing questions when they interfere with the customer's opportunity to reply. Typical kinds of interference include: answering their own questions by hooking their own answers onto the ends of the questions, thereby losing the value of the question; offering the customers alternative answers; not giving the customers time to answer completely; turning questions into statements or explanations, or stringing a group of questions together. Customers should be given time to answer and should not be prompted or interrupted. Bankers should use their judgment in determining how much silence to allow before speaking to fill the void. The danger lies in giving too little time, not too much. Silence can be an effective sales tool for bankers and customers alike, and bankers should learn to use it to their advantage. As for using multiple questions, customers and even bankers themselves cannot keep track of two, three, four, or more questions strung together. Since customers usually answer the last question they hear, important questions can get lost in the crowd. Multiple questions can confuse and even threaten customers and do little to increase the banker's information or control. Bankers should ask one question at a time and wait for an answer. Unless bankers ask one question at a time and patiently and attentively listen to the answers, they might as well not ask them. Another problem with questioning is the reluctance of some bankers to ask questions. Preparation, confidence, and skill can assist bankers in developing and asking questions to gather important information. One skill that assists bankers in feeling more comfortable in asking probing questions is the *prefacing* skill in which bankers introduce the question with a simple explanation as to why the question is being asked. This not only helps bankers feel more comfortable, but also encourages the customer to respond and participate.

Presentation versus Interview

When they fail to use probing questions, bankers engage in monologue presentations. The alternative to the monologue presentation is a sales interview, in which the customer is given an active role in the selling and bankers are frequently rewarded by being given an active part in the decision. In a monologue presentation bankers may monopolize the selling portion of the sale, but customers monopolize the decision portion. In a dialogue both bankers and customers are actively involved throughout the sale.

Summary

Probing questions create an environment in which both the bankers and customers participate in information development and decision making. Questions not only stimulate involvement but also increase the banker's control of the interview. By using open-ended questions to uncover needs, clarify information, redirect discussion, control discussion, and check for understanding and agreement, bankers are in a better position to control not only the sales interview but also the sales results.

When bankers ask questions they must be prepared to listen to the answers. Waiting quietly will encourage customers to respond. Asking probing questions is only part of developing a dialogue; listening to answers is the other part.

Constructive Listening

The Listening Side of Selling

A significant amount of selling takes place when bankers are listening, not talking. Since it is what customers themselves say or think that determines the decision, it is important that customers be given the opportunity to present their ideas. It is only when customers see the value of a product or recognize a need for it themselves that they are motivated to buy. Customers often sell themselves based on the information that they provide to the bankers concerning their own needs and situation. Bankers can help customers sell themselves by listening to find out what is on their minds and using that information in suggesting solutions, improvements, or alternatives. When bankers do most of the talking, they have no way of estimating whether they are on target, whether their ideas are of interest or value to their customers, or whether customers understand and accept their ideas. It is important that bankers give their customers the opportunity to speak and that they focus on the ideas presented.

Most people have not had listening training, and the conversational listening skills that they possess often fall short of the kind of listening skills needed in a selling situation. Constructive listening goes beyond conversational listening. It requires that bankers absorb and use what their customers tell them. It consists, first, of paying attention to the customer, and second, of responding with a comment that incorporates what the customer has said. Unless bankers incorporate and utilize what they hear, they may never demonstrate to the customer that they understand and can satisfy the customer's needs.

Although constructive listening is crucial in need-driven selling, it is not practiced as consistently as it should be. There are a number of reasons for this. Some typical reasons that bankers block out customers when they are talking are that they think they already know what the customer is saying, they are preparing their own responses, they think they are relinquishing control, or they think their customers are wrong.

Whatever the reason, not listening or selective listening during a sales interview will invariably block sales opportunities. For example, even if the customer is making inaccurate statements, without an understanding of the customer's misinformation and misperceptions, bankers will not be in a position to effect corrections.

Bankers should consciously focus on what the customer is saying even if they find it boring or repetitious. Although some customers are easier to listen to than others, all customers must be heard if needs are to be satisfied and sales are to be made. Good listening skills are, however, invaluable in selling situations, and bankers should work toward developing and improving them. Consultative listening requires concentration, attention, and training. Bankers will be rewarded by an increased number of sales, not only difficult sales but also the "easy" sales that turn out to be not so easy because the customer's point of view was not incorporated and his or her confidence was not won.

Constructive Listening Technique

By sitting erect, maintaining eye contact, and taking notes, bankers can improve their concentration. As they concentrate on what customers say, they should store key ideas (words) in their memory bank and construct a mental list. When they respond, bankers should integrate the key words or ideas from their mental list in a positive, supportive way. The word *list* is actually the archaic word for *listen,* and the archaic meaning implies remembering and referring to the information that is recorded. The remembering and referring aspects of the word *listen* are essential in a sales situation.

Constructive listening requires that bankers truly appreciate the value of customer input. Bankers can start their sales off on the right foot by asking probing questions so that the customer will talk about his or her business, ideas, concerns, needs, staffing, or internal operations. While the customer is talking, bankers should be taking mental or written notes and highlighting in their minds the key customer words. As the customer talks, whether it is for two or 20 minutes, bankers should identify the one or several ideas that are important to the customer and should register and sort them mentally. After the customer has stopped talking, bankers should use the items from their list to relate their product information to the customer's needs, ideas, or concerns.

Constructive listening has taken place when bankers:

Comment on general items in which they agree with their customers.

Incorporate key ideas that the customer has presented.

Discuss features and benefits of their products as they relate to the customer's ideas (key words).

Check for agreement and understanding after each item is discussed.

Too often, unfortunately, bankers—and people in general—do just the opposite. When they respond, they begin with the way or ways in which they *disagree* with what has been said. Often they begin their ideas with "No" or "I don't agree." Bankers should train themselves to use the customer's point of view by appreciating what the customer has said (recognizing and referring to it) and in a *positive* way tying it to their product advantages or with new information. They should work with their customers, not against them.

Another problem occurs when customers present several ideas at one time, and bankers focus on the last point or the point that was of interest to them, rather than focusing on the total picture or total list and covering each idea, one at a time. Bankers should train themselves to listen, to sort out points of agreement and disagreement, to keep track of all the key ideas that they hear, to lead with a point of agreement and support, and to cover all of the points presented. For example, in discussing Export Letters of Credit:

Customer.   I'm not too *sure* of the foreign market. We have done *fairly well* with our jeans here and I don't know if we should venture any further. I was in *London* last month and we talked to a bank there, but I'm *not sure.*

Banker.   You *certainly* have done *very well* over the past four years, and I can understand your *hesitance,* since it would be a new market. May I ask to whom you were speaking in *London?*

Customer.   Y Bank, and they went over some procedures with me but I'm *still not sure* it's a good idea. We decided to wait.

Banker.   I think we may be able to help in . . ., but before discussing some alternatives, may I ask what specific concerns you have about . . . in doing business abroad?

Customer.   We've done okay here, but we know our customers. My brother and I built this business up. *How do we know we'll get paid?*

By questioning and listening, the banker in the example was able to uncover the customer's specific concern. The banker developed a selling situation in which he could address and attempt to satisfy a specific concern in a way that the banker from the English bank apparently could not. Throughout the dialogue the banker referred to the key idea expressed by the customer. By incorporating the customer's ideas, the banker showed sensitivity to the customer's concerns, and by listening and probing he was able to narrow down the concern. The banker could then discuss the ways in which her bank could assist the customer in protecting himself and being assured of payment.

Some techniques to use to develop constructive listening skills are the following:

Develop a Mental List of Key Ideas as the Customer Talks. Bankers should listen for key words or cues in what the customer says. By identifying and utilizing key words, bankers can recognize and pursue opportunities. Following are some examples of the kinds of "opportunity phrases" that bankers may extract from the customer's discussion:

"Causing delays"

"My treasurer"

"Problems with our subsidiaries"

"Lack of control"

"Turnover"

"X bank has made a proposal."

"Need for more flexibility"

"Our board"

"Problems with our accountant"

"Have never really thought of you as an international bank"

"Complaints about. . . ."

"We don't have a good handle on our balances."

Expressions like these, as well as many others, should raise red flags in bankers' minds. *Bankers should ask questions to get further clarifications.* The customer's replies may provide bankers with opportunities to solve problems through the bank's credit and noncredit products and services. For instance, the statement "We don't have a *good handle* on our *balances*" should trigger questions concerning idle balances and reporting systems. When the customer has finished talking, the banker might ask, "I know that kind of information is important. So that I can . . . may I ask how you presently get your balance information?" "What problems. . . ?" "How helpful would it be to have a consolidated report . . . to make investment decisions?"

Bankers should cue in to opportunity phrases and pursue them in their responses. Bankers should pay close attention to any words that are emotionally (positively or negatively) charged. General or ambiguous words that customers use can also provide bankers with opportunities. For example, phrases such as "too complicated" or "too time-consuming" need to be explored and discussed. When customers use general or ambiguous terms, bankers' questions may help customers narrow down the concern and define specifically what disturbs them. Bankers need to train themselves to *hear* and *use* what the customer discloses.

Take Notes.   By taking notes, bankers can improve their concentration and increase their ability to keep track of important ideas to be covered. In addition to this, note-taking, at appropriate times, demonstrates interest to customers and an intention to follow through.

Draw from the Mental List When Constructing a Reply.   The mental list may consist of one idea or multiple ideas, depending on what the customer has said. Although it is easier to address one idea at a time, bankers do not have this luxury often, since customers often stick several ideas together. When the customer gives several ideas in one response, it is important to respond to the total picture with a general, positive, supportive comment and then to address each point individually. Use the *customer's words* or at the very least *synonyms* when replying, as a way to tie the product to the customer's needs. When bankers are not certain which point to address first, they can ask the customer by saying, "You have mentioned several important ideas. Which is a priority for . . . ?"

Begin with a Note of Agreement.   A comment that acknowledges or supports what the customer has said provides a way to help the customer become receptive and open to communications. Bankers who can develop this skill in sales situations have a great advantage in communicating. The difference may seem subtle, but it is the difference between being positive or negative. For example, in discussing International Cash Letters:

Negative

Customer.   But you all use the same airplanes?

Banker.   No we don't. We use our own system for scheduling the most timely flights and we . . .

Customer. We are perfectly happy with X Bank and see no reason to jeopardize the relationship for a product that we already have.

Positive

Customer. But you all use the same airplanes?

Banker. It's true that we use the same planes, but because of our attention to flight time, and the processing efficiency and availability we provide, we may be able to offer some improvements. May I ask how satisfied you are with the efficiency of the service you now receive? (Or if availability were the competitive edge, the banker could have asked, "What availability do you receive?")

The banker in the positive example used the customer's idea as a building block rather than contradicting or wiping out what the customer said.

Close Incrementally. Bankers should check for agreement and understanding between themselves and their customers by using probing questions. The·· should confirm agreement or disagreement *before going on to the next point*. For example: "How might our coordination of flight and processing time assist in reducing. . . ?"

Never Interrupt. Bankers must train themselves to listen and to wait until the customer has finished talking. When bankers and customers engage in "overtalk" (talking at the same time) during sales calls, the customer always has the right of way. Bankers should train themselves, literally, to stop talking the very second the customer begins to talk in a sales interview.

   The following examples contrast a segment of a sale without and one with constructive listening.

Eavesdrop on a Sales Interview without Constructive Listening

Customer: We sell soft goods in Japan. We bill our customer in dollars, and the amount of the receipts varies considerably. It's hard for us to forecast revenues. It's hard to know what our income is likely to be. We bill in dollars because it is more convenient, since we don't know much about Foreign Exchange.

Banker.   We suggest that you hedge your yen exposure by using a forward contract.

Customer.   Wait a minute. We don't know anything about Foreign Exchange. I don't want to speculate, and I know that my president doesn't want me to speculate.

Banker.   I don't think you can call this speculating.

Analysis. The customer's and banker's ideas are clashing. What went wrong? The banker did not refer to the customer's problem but rather rushed the solution and contradicted the customer.

Eavesdrop on a Sales Interview with Constructive Listening

Customer.   We sell soft goods in Japan. We bill our customers in dollars and the amount of receipts varies considerably. It's hard for us to forecast revenues. It's hard to know what our income is likely to be. We bill in dollars because it is more convenient, since we don't know much about Foreign Exchange.

Banker.   Managing Foreign Exchange exposure does require some expertise. What specific concerns do you have about your invoicing to Japan?

Customer.   I want to protect my profits. The way it is working now, *we don't know what we'll get for our dollars.*

Banker.   *Not knowing what you'll get for the dollars* is a real problem. Would it be helpful if we could work out a way to eliminate the fluctuations and uncertainty of payment? Perhaps we can help you lock in what you will be getting and protect your profits.

Customer.   It certainly would.

Banker.   We have a way to guarantee you a predetermined rate for your yen, and you wouldn't have to worry about the fluctuations. By using a forward contract, you could be assured of a fixed price so that you would know exactly how much you would be paid. You could base your costs and contracts on that fixed price. You are a dollar-based company, and you need to know easily the amount you are going to get. You can invoice in yen and we can advise you on. . . . You could set your costs in advance and . . . profits. . . . How might that help?

Customer. It sounds like a good approach, but we don't want to speculate.

Banker. I can see why you would not want to speculate. But by using a forward contract in which. . . , you would in fact be eliminating risk. . . .

Analysis. With constructive listening, banker and customer are in sync. This banker constructively listened to what the customer said. She utilized the information in constructing her responses and began to work toward building agreement.

Summary

Dialogue is critical to consultative selling, and listening is one half of the dialogue process. Too often bankers monopolize the sale. There should be an equal-time clause in all sales interviews, to ensure that there are both customer and banker input. One of the saddest commentaries on a lost sale is: "The customer just didn't understand." Bankers have the responsibility to help customers understand how their product will benefit the customer. When the customer does not understand, it is usually because bankers have not listened and thus did not understand which specific aspects confused or concerned the customer. Unless bankers can look at their products through their *customer's eyes,* they will not succeed in satisfying needs and selling the products. The only way to understand the customer's points of view is to encourage discussion. Bankers can identify specific concerns by asking probing questions and listening to customers' responses. Unless customers are given the opportunity to discuss their thoughts, bankers will not be in a position to satisfy their needs or concerns.

Features and Benefits

Feature–Benefit Strategy

After the customer's Motivation Lever has been identified, bankers can use the feature–benefit strategy to discuss products or services as they relate to the customer's situation. Although the feature–benefit approach is not new, it remains the most effective way to understand and discuss a product for selling purposes.

It is impossible to understand a product without understanding the features of the product. *Features* are the traits, attributes, or qualities that the bank puts into the product to make it function. Features are the "nuts and bolts" of the product or service. When discussed without their corresponding benefits, however, they can lack appeal in a selling situation. *Benefits* are the values the customer derives from the product. Benefits point out to the customer how it may be possible to increase profits, reduce clerical expense, and maximize opportunities. Too often, bankers do not discuss benefits because they assume that the customer understands the benefits; they think that discussing them would be redundant, unnecessary, pushy, or hard sell, or they simply do not know them (trained only in operational aspects of the product). This is unfortunate, since *customers buy benefits.* Customers usually are interested in the bank's products not for academic reasons but rather for the ways in which the bank's products can meet their needs. Customers are constantly evaluating *what is in a bank's proposition, deal, or product for them.* It is the banker's responsibility to identify the customer's needs and convey how those needs can be satisfied.

Linking Features to Benefits

Features and benefits should complement one another. By linking features to their benefits, bankers can stimulate interest and help the customer appreciate the product relative to his or her own situation. When bankers discuss the features of the product to the exclusion of benefits, they are in danger of falling into the "nuts and bolts" trap, in which they risk boring their customers with what appears to be information not related to the customer's needs. Linking features to benefits increases bankers' ability to capture the customer's attention, satisfy customer needs, and establish credibility. Benefits are important because customers buy them. Synonyms for *feature* are *trait, characteristic, attribute, detail, aspect,* and *element;* synonyms for *benefit* are *value, advantage,* and *reward.* Which have more selling power, features or benefits? Of course, benefits do. Benefits alone, however, are not sufficient; they are incomplete when they are used alone. For benefits to be believed, they must be supported by and *linked* to their corresponding features. A benefit cannot exist without a corresponding feature, and one feature may have several benefits. Benefits are the value derived by the customer from the feature. Confidence men make a living selling benefits for which no features exist. Bankers, whose credibility and reputation are of the highest order, can help their customers have *justified confidence* in a product by linking features to benefits.

Here is an example of the feature–benefit strategy for an Import Letter of Credit:

Feature	Benefits
X Bank substitutes its credit standing for that of its customer.	Increases the customer's ability to do business abroad, since the Letter of Credit assures the supplier of payments.
	Strengthens the customer's ability to negotiate price and terms because of assurance of payment.
	Conserves working capital by eliminating the need to pay cash in advance.
	Broadens the customer's sources of supply.
	Enables customers to meet a supplier's request for payment via Letter of Credit.

The following example illustrates how the feature–benefit strategy can help the customer understand the product value of a foreign exchange service.

When a banker explained that her bank's foreign exchange trading and salespeople were located together on the same banking floor, the customer stared blankly. This feature had little appeal to the customer, since he could not see how the physical arrangement of the foreign exchange area could benefit him.

This internal setup would have had much more appeal had the banker linked the benefits to the feature by adding, "This free flow of information will save you time and provide you with up-to-the-minute information, since our salespeople . . . changing rates and conditions."

Feature–benefit selling enables bankers to *relate* the product to customer needs by demonstrating the *responsiveness* of the product to the customer's situation. Regardless of how on line, superior, or advanced a product's technology is, it is of little or no interest to customers unless they understand how it will meet their needs or improve their situation. The feature–benefit approach helps bankers communicate value to customers. Many experienced bankers report that there is nothing more useful in talking "product" with customers than the feature–benefit approach.

Each product has a number of features and benefits. Through questioning bankers can identify which specific benefits respond to the customer's Motivation Lever and are apt to spark and sustain customer interest.

Summary

By taking the time to understand both the features and the benefits of a product, by consciously linking them during a sales call, and by focusing on the particular features and benefits that relate to customer needs, bankers can help satisfy customer needs and expand the market share of the bank. Features and benefits are the heart of sales-oriented product knowledge. They should be used to explain, discuss, or describe a product. They enable bankers to relate what the bank puts into a product to what the customer will get out of it!

Objections

Objections as Sales Opportunities

Objections are an expected and important part of every sales interview. Bankers should understand the relationship between objections and opportunities, and use them to satisfy needs and concerns. When they are resolved, objections can provide bankers with a way to advance in the sale; when they cannot be fielded successfully, they can block opportunities. If the objection cannot be offset by the product's total offer or product's options, bankers should recognize this barrier and save valuable time. *Objections are negative when they block what should have been viable sales opportunities.*

Customers object for a host of reasons. Some customers may be testing bankers, testing their competence, or being contrary or difficult. Some may object because they are apprehensive about making a decision or fear making a wrong decision; others may lack technical knowledge or authority to make the decision and be reluctant to admit it.

Although there are probably as many reasons for customer objections as there are customers, there are essentially two kinds of objections. The first is the genuine objection. Genuine objections are made by customers who honestly do not understand the product. If the banker had the same misperceptions or lack of information about the product as this kind of customer, the banker would also object! The second kind of objection is the "role" or "staged" objection. Role objections are used by experienced customers to test the banker's knowledge and check professionalism or competence. Such customers see as a part of their role as customer the need to go through a scenario, most of which is already well known. This, they believe, is the way to do their job and make a decision with confidence. Role objections occur frequently in negotiations in which both seller and customer are required to assume roles. Frequently after a heated but resolved negotiation a customer will say, "You really did a great job," to which the banker will respond in a positive and appreciative way, "You weren't so bad yourself!" Nevertheless, whether objections are genuine or staged, bankers should take objections seriously and work toward resolving them. Both kinds of objections are an important part of selling.

Regardless of their motivations, customers' objections are valid and must be fielded by bankers if sales opportunities are to be realized. To exploit the positive opportunities in objections, bankers should consider *all* objections as *signals* from the customer for more information or clarification. The underlying reason for most customer objections is a *need for more information* concerning the value or benefits of the product. Unless bankers can resolve objections, they may lose viable opportunities to complete sales or make quality referrals to specialists.

Product knowledge, linking features to benefits, is of course essential in overcoming objections, but it is not enough. In addition to having the product knowledge necessary to address the objections, bankers should be able to *communicate information* without directly affronting, confronting, contradicting, offending, or frightening the customers. When handled properly, objections can be used as a ladder for making the sale, since each objection can be an opportunity to inform the customer and to build rapport and establish credibility.

Objection Response Model

The way in which an objection is handled is as important as what is said. The Objection Response Model provides a process for resolving all kinds of objections. It is a process that bankers can use to turn many objections into selling points. The Objection Response Model is a vehicle through which bankers can effectively communicate their product information. It consists of the following four basic steps:

1 *Repeat the Objection and Show Empathy.*   Rephrasing or restating the objection assures the customer that his or her objection was heard. It shows *empathy* for the customer's irritation or concern and reduces the customer's defensiveness and aggression. By defusing the objection and soothing customer hostility, bankers can prepare customers at least to listen to the bankers' replies. Restating the objection also provides bankers with a moment to compose their thoughts. It helps bankers approach a negative situation from a positive point of view and reframe the negativity.

2 *Ask a Clarifying Question When Objection Is Vague.*   The majority of objections are general. Clarifying or narrowing down an objection renders it more manageable. It is almost impossible to satisfy a vague or general objection. For example, if the customer objects to the bank's Account Reconcilement System by saying, "Those systems have too many problems!" the banker's response should include, "I can appreciate your caution, but *what specific problems are of concern to you?*" By qualifying or narrowing the objection, the banker can address specific concerns and work toward satisfying them. If the customer reveals a concern about lost checks, the bank's new automated system, with a built-in verification mechanism and special check location coding, may satisfy that concern. Another example would be a customer who says, "I did not receive my account analysis" or "My statement is always late." Bankers should respond, "I'm sorry that there seems to be a problem. Could you give me specific dates so that I could look into this immediately?" Also, for the customer who says, "X Bank says your cash management system is the most expensive," bankers could reply, "Cost of course is a consideration. May I ask what specific products they were discussing? Who . . . ?"

By showing concern for the customer and narrowing the objections, bankers are in a better position to satisfy them.

3 *Present Product Knowledge.* Bankers should use their product knowledge to satisfy customer concerns. Objections provide bankers with an opportunity to discuss the capabilities of the product and to help the customer appreciate the value that he or she can derive from it. Bankers should use objections as opportunities to enlighten and inform customers, in a clear and relevant way.

4 *Use the Incremental Close.* Each time bankers respond to an objection, they should *check* with the customer to find out, *whether the answer satisfied the concern.* By using open-ended questions to close incrementally, bankers can check for comprehension and agreement before proceeding to another point. The incremental close serves as a barometer for the sales call by checking on the extent to which the customer understands and accepts the bankers' ideas and information. It assists bankers in determining their next step (whether to proceed in the sale, backtrack, or switch gears.) An example of an incremental close is: "How does our ability to trade in all major currencies, including . . . , satisfy your concern about our scope?" During the incremental close, it is what the customer, not the banker, says that is important.

Bankers who do not use the Objection Response Model often find themselves in a "yes–no" match with their customers. By applying the Objection Response Model, bankers can turn objections into positive selling points.

The specific words or phrases that bankers select are a matter of professional and personal style; nothing should be done to interfere with or replace their individuality. On paper the model may appear rigid, but when the words and tone are chosen by bankers to suit their conversational styles, the model becomes invisible. It is a process, not a script. The model is effective in reducing customer resistance and in assisting bankers in communicating their ideas. Unfortunately many bankers attempt to field objections by giving product knowledge without taking the time to repeat and clarify the objection. Then after they discuss their product and information, they fail to check for understanding and agreement on the customer's part, and therefore are not as effective as they could be. Bankers should experiment with the Objection Response Model in nonbusiness as well as business situations to determine its effectiveness in improving communications and establishing agreement or clarity. The Objection Response Model provides a communication *process* for satisfying objections by understanding and clarifying the objection and testing for understanding and acceptance from the customer.

Of course, before any objection can be resolved, it must be understood. As soon as the customer begins to object, bankers should stop talking. Besides being courteous, this indicates concern for the customer and avoids overtalk. By being quiet, bankers can encourage the customer to express his or her concern or criticism. Bankers should listen carefully to the *complete* objection. By giving the customer time to elaborate on the objection, bankers can gain valuable insight into the customer's thinking, which they can then use in formulating their responses.

The four steps of the Objection Response Model provide the foundation for turning objections into sale opportunities. Some experienced bankers say that they can benchmark the progress of the sale by the sequence and handling of objections. The Objection Response Model is designed to provide empathy (repeat objection), clarity (clarifying question), data (product knowledge), and customer feedback (incremental close). It should be used by bankers whenever they face a significant objection.

Bankers should welcome objections as opportunities to look at the product from the customer's point of view. Unless bankers are willing to look at the product from the customer's perspective, they should not be surprised with the customer's reluctance, refusal, or inability to understand the benefits of the product as the banker sees them. The Objection Response Model puts bankers in a better position to establish an *advocate* rather than a neutral or adversary role. As advocates or consultants they can work with the customer toward developing mutually beneficial relationships. Bankers have the best opportunities for success when they understand their customer's point of view before they try to promote their own. Customers are more willing to work with bankers who are trying to solve problems than with bankers who are trying to sell products.

Objections are one of the best ways bankers have of seeing the product or situation as the customer sees it. It is the responsibility of bankers to help the customer appreciate the value of the product, but unless they appreciate the customer's perceptions or misperceptions, they cannot work toward changing them.

The Objection Response Model is designed to improve communications at crucial moments throughout the sale. If bankers cannot overcome, offset, or neutralize objections, they risk losing the opportunity to complete the sale or make a referral to a product specialist. When customers object, they are in a negative mode. As bankers respond to objections, they work toward establishing a positive mode. Unless bankers succeed in restoring a positive environment, sparks will fly, and although bankers may win a point, they may lose the sale or the relationship. It is important that bankers utilize objections as opportunities to sell. Bankers should combine sales-oriented product knowledge (features and benefits) with effective communication skills (Objection Response Model). Regardless of how accurate the product content of the bankers' responses may be, unless it is communicated in a positive way, customers will not fully accept the information, or they will seek an alternative banking source whenever one is available.

The Challenge of Objections

The Objection Response Model is the basic strategy for resolving objections that can threaten an opportunity. Bankers should be prepared to withstand the challenge of objections. They should expect the following objections as a sign of a viable sale.

Price/Terms Objections

Resistance to Price.   Bankers continuously face the price objection, "Your price is too high!" Price objections are inevitable regardless of price. Customers often say, "The price is too high" or "You're too expensive" even before price is discussed.

Bankers should expect and be prepared for price resistance. Price objections are often closing signals from the customer. If they are not fielded properly, or if they are addressed prematurely by bankers, viable opportunities can be lost. Failing to satisfy price objections results not only in loss of sales but also in a loss of morale for bankers.

Price Traps.   When bankers are fielding price objections, they are in the *negotiating* phase of the sale. It is a high-intensity phase that requires control, skill, and preparation if sales opportunities are to be realized.

Unless handled properly, price objections can lead bankers into price traps. Bankers fall into price traps when they make excuses for the prices or blame someone else, rather than exploring and addressing the objections and comparing value.

Typical price trap responses are:

Customer. Your price is too high.
Banker. *We have to make a profit too.*

Customer. Your price is too high.
Banker. *You're right, but I'm just told what they are.*

Customer. Your price is too high.
Banker. *My hands are tied. With the cost of money to us, what else can we do?*

Customer. Your price is too high.
Banker. *For a company of your size, this is the figure.*

Customer. Your price is too high.
Banker. *Well, we can lower it.*

Customer. Your price is too high.
Banker. *No it isn't. X Bank . . . !*

Customer. Your price is too high.
Banker. *I don't have the authority to change it.*

Customer. Your price is too high.
Banker. *So is everyone else's.*

Customer. Your price is too high.
Banker. *We accept balances.*

Customer. Your price is too high.
Banker. *You get what you pay for.*

These responses put the deal in jeopardy. They place the banker in an argumentative, defensive, weak, or at best neutral position. Each response takes the price objection at its face value, rather than understanding the reasoning behind it and comparing alternatives and value. *Each time one of these phrases is uttered by bankers, a sales opportunity is in danger* of being lost. Rather than defending the price, transferring the blame to the bank, the marketplace, the customer, or the competition, or rushing to change the price or conditions, bankers should acknowledge the price objection, *explore* it with the customer, and evaluate it to compare total value. Giving the customer the opportunity to explain his or her objection does not amplify it; having a customer explain his or her objection is the first step in satisfying it! An effective way to avoid the price traps is to utilize the *Total Offer approach*. The Total Offer enables bankers to understand the objection and to discuss it relative to total comparative value to the customer. It often helps customers sell themselves as they answer their own objection.

Total Offer Approach. The Total Offer will help bankers avoid being trapped and defeated by price objections by encouraging the customer to appreciate price–value. The Total Offer consists of two parts:

1   Finding out what the customer is comparing the product, deal, or service to in considering it too expensive: "What are you *comparing* it to in considering it too expensive?" (Comparison is the key!) *or* "In *relation to what* do you consider the cost to be too high?"
2   Making a comparison of the bank's total product, ideal, or service with other alternatives: "I think if we compare total packages you may find. . . ."

By making a comparison, bankers and customers can evaluate alternatives, cost, and value. To employ the Total Offer, bankers must understand *what their products are being compared to,* so that they can discuss cost relative to value (compare apples with apples, not apples with oranges). Bankers should help customers compare values, and to do this they must uncover details about competitive offers (another bank) or the alternatives (in-house system) the customer is considering. Without the Total Offer, bankers may find themselves involved in a comparison of unequal offers, in which their price may be justifiably higher because their product is superior in customer value. Often if bankers were to trim off the additional features for deals in which their price is higher, their price would be comparable. This, however, often results in trimming off benefits that are important to the customer. Competitive offers or products can *appear* to be comparable on the surface, but by exploring the specific *features* and *benefits* or *requirements of the competitors* bankers may uncover substantial differences in the value and in the ability of the products to satisfy customer needs.

Although the Total Offer is a technique for responding to all price objections, it is especially valuable in situations in which the bank appears to have a higher price or in which the bank's price is in fact higher. By comparing the bank's package with that of a competitor, bankers can often demonstrate that although the products *appear* to be the same, the total packages may be significantly different. By pointing out additional features and benefits that are of value to the customer, by examining compensating balances or qualifying criteria, and by comparing the total relative value of products, bankers may show that the price difference represents value differences. The Total Offer is designed to protect the bank's profit while demonstrating to the customer the value to him or her. The Total Offer (in comparison to what?) is the most effective way to field price objections and build mutually profitable long-term relationships.

The Total Offer capitalizes on the fact that price is a major but *not* all-important factor considered by the customer in his or her decision to buy. To keep price in its proper perspective bankers should discuss price in terms of the Total Offer. The Total Offer could include:

Quality of service

Guarantee of performance

Expertise

Professionalism

Personal commitment

Length/strength of ties to bank

Innovation

State of art

Ability to customize

Prestige

Future relationship
Visibility in the bank

Of course, ideas such as these should not be presented as a laundry list, but should be tailored and used selectively with each customer. If the banker is selling to a relationship-oriented customer (not a transactional customer who can be a good customer whose style is to "shop"), certain aspects of the bank's package are most likely to apply. Bankers should never discuss price until all of the relevant features and benefits of the deal are understood by the customer and then they should do so in terms of the Total Offer.

The Total Offer technique also helps bankers withstand customer pressure strategies, in which customers attempt to test bankers by alluding to nonexistent competitive offers or alternatives. Bankers who ask for specifics concerning the other offer are less susceptible to such pressure strategies. By politely asking customers for specifics, bankers can help customers realistically evaluate their alternatives. By using the total offer, bankers can politely test a customer's sincerity and the accuracy of his or her information.

Cushion Approach.   When discussing price, bankers can also use the cushion approach to convey confidence as they state the price. The cushion approach utilizes timing, tone of voice, and knowledge of key benefits. Bankers often unintentionally communicate a lack of confidence in their price by pausing before and after they state the price and by lowering their voices or inflecting the end of the word as they state the price. For example, they might say, "X%" with their voices going up on the word percent followed by a pause in which they seem to be waiting for the boom to be lowered by the customer, as it frequently is.

It may be more effective for bankers consciously to avoid this delay or pause by introducing price with a key benefit, immediately following the price with an additional or special benefit that the bankers have been saving—hence cushioning the price.

Premature Price Objections.   Specific needs and requirements as well as bank capabilities should be understood before price is discussed or before price objections are addressed. Before fielding price objections, bankers should determine whether they are advanced enough in the sale to discuss price accurately. Banking products are often complicated because they contain options. Unless bankers understand the *customer's specific requirements* and have determined and fully discussed the features and benefits that will accrue to the customer, they cannot properly or accurately discuss a price or respond to price objections. Price objections can be fielded successfully only when the value is fully understood by the customer. Customers who say, "Just tell me the price, before anything else," are frequently more than willing to *delay* discussing price if the delay is justified by the need to find out the customer's specific requirements so that accurate prices can be quoted. Bankers must recognize such situations and say, "Yes, so that we can discuss price, let's look at the specifics of your requirements. What . . . ?" A rule of thumb is that price should not be discussed until there is a time investment (allowing for information and interest) on the customer's part.

Pricing is really the negotiating part of the sale. Uncovering needs, explaining the product, and establishing the desire and securing the decision to buy are *selling*. Settling on rate, price or terms is *negotiating*. Selling sets the tone, readiness, and commitment for the negotiations. The selling phase is broad, identifying needs and requirements, but the negotiating phase is highly focused, shaping the terms of the agreement. When pricing comes up too early, bankers should use the inquiry about price as an opportunity to gather specific information. This takes some courage at first, but when handled politely and consultatively, bankers can strengthen their position.

Although bankers should always be given pricing information on all products, there are times when they should not discuss price during a sales call since the price is negotiable based on conditions, options, or the customer relationship or profitability. In a situation in which the matter of price should be deferred to a product specialist, bankers should use the customer's question or objection about price as a lead-in to setting the appointment with a specialist.

Sometimes bankers are tempted to give ballpark figures or ranges. Although this may be necessary, it can be dangerous, since customers will hear the low side. One of the best ways to defer discussing a price is to state that it is competitive and suggest setting an appointment with a specialist who could discuss price based on the customer's requirements, his or her credit situation, or the total relationship with the bank.

Price Trauma. Price is a sensitive issue even when the product involved is of the finest quality and bankers have confidence in the quality and pricing of their products. Even some bankers who have confidence in their bank's products shudder when price is mentioned. *They often assume that any question or mention of price is an objection.* This "price trauma" is preconditioned. Since banking has become such a competitive and volatile industry, bankers are continuously being bombarded with pricing complaints and objections. But bankers should remember that price is one of the many *features* of their products. They should address questions about price as they would about any feature—by linking it to its benefit—and they should use the Objection Response Model when price objections occur. They should discuss price by linking the cost with value. Bankers equipped to field price objections in a consultative manner have an advantage in responding to and satisfying the objection because they can assist the customer in appreciating the value to him or her.

Confidence in Pricing. In resolving price objections, bankers should have confidence in the value and merit of their product and its ability to assist the customer. If bankers do not believe in their bank's products or pricing policy, it will show, and they won't be able to maximize selling and cross-selling opportunities. Without confidence and respect for their products and pricing, bankers can be their own worst enemies, because their lack of confidence will be conveyed to the customer. Too often bankers believe that their products are not competitive in price or quality. Often the data from which they draw conclusions are hearsay; in many situations competitors' products are *similar*—not identical—in price and quality. There are in fact substantial differences in the capabilities and operations of most bank's products, contrary to the myth that all bank's products are the same; competitor banks are simply unable to ascertain one another's differences. If bankers assume that their products are not competitive, or that the pricing for a product is out of line relative to competitive prices, they should channel this feedback to their managers so that the information can be verified or the misperceptions can be corrected and, when necessary, the products can be improved. Feedback from bankers can be used to initiate product improvements and verify or correct internal and external perceptions. Misperceptions from the field must be corrected if the sales force is to function in a confident and aggressive way. When perceptions are correct and products are not competitive in price, value, or hardware, banks must correct the situation or face the price they will have to pay in lost opportunities for having noncompetitive products. No amount of product knowledge or consultative selling skills can consistently compensate for a product that is not competitive in price and value or a sales force that does not believe in its product. The bank and bankers alike should take the time and energy to find out about their competitors' products if they are to succeed in the highly competitive market environment.

Competitive Objections

There are two kinds of competitive objections: "the other offer" and "my present bank."

The Other Offer.   The "other offer" objection is similar to the price objection, except that the customer objects by referring to a better offer made by a competitor bank. The Objection Response Model and the Total Offer technique should also be used to field all competitive objections. It is *impossible* for bankers to respond to a competitive objection *unless they know the specifics of the other offer* or of the alternatives under consideration. By asking, "Could you tell me a little about their offer so that we can compare service and pricing?" or "You mentioned that X Bank has an attractive package; what in particular did you find of interest to you?" or "You mentioned you were speaking to another bank; may I ask . . . ?" bankers can retain control, while helping customers evaluate their options. If the customer is using the competitive objection as a pressure strategy, the Total Offer assists bankers in testing and withstanding the objection. When the customer states that he or she has a competitive offer or is looking at the competition, *bankers must make an attempt to get the specifics of the offer* or find out as much as possible about the alternatives that the customer is considering, particularly the active competition, so that they can construct their package accordingly and also so that they can assist the customer in comparing and evaluating their added value.

To field competitive objections successfully, bankers require up-to-date competitive information. When bank intelligence cannot provide specific competitive information or cannot supplement in-house information, bankers should gather competitive information from another excellent source, their customers. Bankers who ask, "What alternatives are you considering?'' or ''What's in their deal?'' often gather a wealth of useful information that they can use to help their customers compare and evaluate alternatives. They should also remember to ask, ''When did they [are they] make [making] the presentation?'' ''What is your time frame for making a decision?''

My Present Bank. Today many companies are overbanked, and when bankers approach a prospect they are advised that the prospect's present bank handles everything for him or her. Bankers faced with a ''my present bank'' objection should be prepared to inquire politely about the specifics of what the other bank is providing. Their rationale for this is to assist the customer in comparing and evaluating his or her present banking situation to determine whether there are any possible advantages in utilizing another bank to supplement the present service. For example, if a multinational company is using X Bank's Balance Reporting System, the banker can inquire about the timeliness and quality of the reporting and the kinds of reports provided. By identifying the competitor banker, and by knowing competitive information, the banker can ask questions to point out areas for possible opportunities and improvements. For example:

Customer. X Bank is our lead bank and they provide our balance reporting.

Banker. I respect your relationship with them. To determine whether there are any possible advantages that we may have that could supplement the information you receive, may I ask how you . . .?

Inherent Objections

Every product and every bank have inherent objections. The advantage of these objections is that they can be anticipated and prepared for. Bankers can take advantage of the *predictability* of certain objections by developing the key points to be covered in responding to them. For example, when discussing Import Letter of Credit, bankers frequently hear:

''We use documentary collections.''

''We pay everything by check.''

''It involves too much paper work.''

A discussion of Automated Payroll often includes:

"We would spend *more* time filling out *your* forms."

"I don't want to drive downtown just to drop my payroll."

"I use another service."

"We do it in house."

"It's too expensive." (Price objections are inherent in almost every product.)

Objections that frequently accompany an Account Reconcilement sales call are:

"We have our own system."

"Account Rec systems have too many errors."

"Our volume isn't large enough."

Other common objections include:

"We'll lose our float." (Direct Deposit of Payroll)

"You're not on our list." (Commercial Paper)

"Your rate is too high." (Loan, Commercial, or Personal)

"My customers will object." (Preauthorized Checks)

"There is a danger of unauthorized transfers." (Wire Transfers)

By anticipating the objections and preparing their responses *before* the sales call, bankers can use their product knowledge to turn objections into selling points. They should field these objections using their product knowledge and the Objection Response Model. Product knowledge, pre-sales-call homework, and experience assist bankers in anticipating objections and resolving them. The banker's responses can provide customers with the information necessary to reevaluate the objection. Customers can utilize the information to evaluate their own needs and possible advantages. For example:

Product: Account Reconcilement	***Objection Response Model***
Customer. We have an in-house system.	
Banker. I can appreciate the work involved in organizing an effective system and your not wanting to disturb it without substantial benefits. Could you tell me a little about your system so that we can determine what possible advantages there may be in . . . ? How do you reconcile your account?	Repeat objection. / Clarify question.
Customer. We have three clerks. . . .	
Banker. What problems . . . ?	
Customer. . . . workload control.	
Banker. We may have a way to alleviate the tedious monthly checking account balancing and reduce clerical and administrative cost . . . control over check disbursement . . . What are your thoughts on simplifying the reconcilements by . . .?	Link features to benefits. / Close incrementally.

If bankers allow themselves to be deterred by objections without giving a second effort, they may well lose opportunities in which both the customer and the bank could profit. By being prepared for inherent objections and successfully resolving them, bankers can consult with their customers and increase market share.

Bad-Experience Objections

If the customer has had a negative experience with a product, service, bank, or banker, he or she may automatically reject the banker's ideas because of that experience. Bankers should show empathy and get the specifics of the experience and determine the extent to which the situation has been remedied or changed. The "not true now" technique is very helpful in situations in which a problem existed in the past but has been corrected. This acknowledges the existence of the problem and addresses the *changes* that have been made to improve the situation.

Bankers should be prepared for these objections and utilize the Objection Response Model and "not true now" technique.

Customer.	I wouldn't bank with you!	
Banker.	I'm sorry to hear that. Could you tell me why you feel that way?	Repeat objection and seek clarification.
Customer.	Two years ago we came to you. . . .	
Banker.	Your reaction is understandable, and I regret that the situation occurred. At that time, we. . . . Today our management recognizes. . . . My specific assignment reflects this, and perhaps. . . . What are your thoughts on . . . ?	Use "not true now" technique. Close incrementally.

By facing the objection in a consultative manner, bankers are in a position to *acknowledge the particular problem, express concern, discuss the changes,* and *work toward reestablishing credibility and building a relationship.*

"What-If" Objections

Customers often require reassurance in making decisions and seek answers to "what-if" situations as a way to feel more confident. Case histories are confidence builders. They enable bankers to document results and add credibility to their proposals. Bankers can be specific or general in utilizing the case history technique. When a specific case history is used, bankers should refer to customers who are respected in the industry and who have given permission to be used as references. References should also parallel the new customer or prospect in type of business, size, and so on. For example, in response to the objection to using a regional bank for Foreign Exchange transactions, bankers can cite an example appropriate to the customer, either a company, such as a national chain, or a private firm, such as a local museum for whom they do spot trades and forward contracts in several major currencies. Bankers can also use general statements such as "It has been my epxerience," "Most of our customers find . . . ," or "We have found . . . " to build confidence.

Ordeal of Change Objections

When a customer rejects the banker's ideas because he or she is comfortable with the system he or she has been using for years, bankers should use the "what has been your experience . . . ?" technique. Bankers should find out as much as they can about the customer's present situation or system *before* discussing, comparing, or promoting a change to their bank's product. Unless bankers do this they will lack the basis on which to draw comparisons, make suggestions, or successfully point out benefits. It is senseless for bankers ever to suggest that they can do something better, cheaper, or more efficiently, without understanding specifically what it is they will be improving. Consider this discussion of the Import Letter or Credit:

Customer.	I simply pay everything by check.	
Banker.	The check is an appropriate means of making payments, especially domestically. May I ask what has been your experience with operational delays until the check has cleared?	Repeat objection. Seek clarification.
Customer.	When we work with new suppliers and some old ones it can cause some delays. For instance, our holiday decorations arrived in January.	
Banker.	A deal like that must have been frustrating. An alternative such as a Letter of Credit might help reduce problems like that, because the seller is assured of prompt payment after shipment. Letters of Credit motivate the supplier to ship goods on time because documents received after the expiration date may not be accepted. Also, with a Letter of Credit you would not be risking your money in advance of shipment. How helpful would it be . . . ?	Link features to benefits. Close incrementally.
Customer.	I think it might make sense, but what . . . ?	

If there were no delay problems, bankers might ask about control over proper shipment, increasing supplier base, or negotiating terms to find out whether the Import Letter of Credit could benefit the customer. By finding out about the customer's present situation, bankers can consult with him or her about alternatives that wouldd benefit both the customer and the bank. Bankers who do not take the time to understand the customer's needs before selling will find themselves "hard selling."

Smoke-Screen Objections

Smoke-screen objections are those used by customers to mask their real objections. Unless bankers unearth the hidden objections, they may find themselves responding to shadows rather than the customer's real needs. By using probing questions and asking "why" in a consultative manner, bankers can often bring out the hidden objection, address it, or save valuable time. For example:

Customer. Let me think about it. (classic smoke-screen objection)

Banker. This is an important consideration to your company. What specific areas do you want to consider? Perhaps I can provide some additional information.

Customer. It's not that I need more information; I want to pass it by our corporate treasurer.

Banker. That sounds like a good idea. What do you think your treasurer's response will be? What are your thoughts on my meeting with the two of you [or the treasurer] to . . . ?

By gently asking questions to test the objection, bankers can often secure information relative to the genuine objection that will help them stay in the sale.

Vague Objections

Bankers who are confronted by objections often rush to provide an answer even when the objection is vague or general and simply too broad to resolve. The rush may be fatal! Bankers may indeed provide an answer, but the answer may not be remotely related to the customer's concern.

Before answering a broad objection, it is important to find out the specifics. This not only enables the banker to understand the objection and therefore have a chance at resolving it successfully, but it also gives the customer the opportunity to voice any concerns and thereby be *more* open to the banker's reply.

Since it is virtually impossible to satisfy a general objection, bankers must have specifics *before* they respond to it. The "why" technique is particularly useful here. It can change the course of a discussion from negative to positive. It can open doors and reduce defenses. Using the "why" technique enables bankers to understand the specifics of the customer's objections and thus grasp what is really bothering the customer. By narrowing down the objection and responding to the customer's explanations, bankers can position themselves on the customer's side rather than on "the other" side. As he or she explains why, the customer often begins to satisfy or answer his or her own objection or to reveal a further hidden objection. For example:

Customer. Our employees would never accept Direct Deposit.

Banker. I can appreciate your concern for your employees' preferences. But *why* do you think they would resist?

Customer. They have a right to choose their own bank. They don't want us telling them where to bank, and I don't think we should!

Banker. We at X Bank agree with that, and although there are additional benefits to employees who choose us, employees can have their net pay deposited to *any* financial institution in the country that participates in the Automated Clearing House. Our specialists will provide active support in encouraging your employees to accept the plan. How does that address your concerns for your employees' banking choices?

The "why" technique can even assist bankers in fielding one of the most difficult credit-related objections: "I don't want to give my personal guarantee." By asking why rather than explaining to the customer that it is required by bank policy, or offering some similar reason, bankers can often get information that they can use in successfully resolving the objection. Also, by asking why, bankers can avoid making *costly assumptions* that may result in answers that substantiate the customer's objection rather than resolving it. A well-positioned, consultative "why" is unfortunately one of the most underutilized words in sales. "Why" can make bankers aware of the customer's needs, concerns, and goals, and thus can produce new data that can significantly reshape the deal. "Why" can also be a time saver; if a customer has a substantial reason that cannot be offset by the total offer, bankers can recognize the situation early and save valuable time. Consider this discussion of Direct Deposit Payroll:

Customer.   We can't use Direct Deposit here.

Banker.   Why is that, Mr. Smith?

Customer.   On two given weeks *none* of our paychecks are the same, and we change them up to 12 hours before.

Banker.   (The banker's product knowledge of qualifying criteria tells him that his bank requires two-day lead time.) Then your payroll doesn't lend itself to Direct Deposit. Your payroll sounds rather complicated, and perhaps it could be demanding on your and your staff. How do you handle it?

The banker did not belabor Direct Deposit but began to explore Payroll, a new possibility.

Bank Image Objection

Almost all banks are targets for the Bank Image Objection. Bankers must respond to objections based on earnings, size (too big or too small), location, the fact that they are regional or a money center operations (manual or automated), management, "the article in . . . ," merger rumors, and so on before they can accomplish anything else. When the objection is basically one that is widely recognized, such as earnings, bankers should acknowledge the concern and briefly discuss the bank's position. When the situation has been or is about to be improved, bankers should document the improvement.

When the objection is more subjective, such as regional versus money-center banking, bankers should capitalize on the strengths of their position and describe their advantage, whether it is personal attention (small) or an international correspondent network (large), to assist customers in appreciating the particular value to them. For all subjective Bank Image Objections there are usually two sides, and bankers should be prepared to accentuate the strength of their side.

With all Bank Image Objections, bankers should work toward increasing the customer's confidence in the bank. The best way to achieve this is through a prepared and responsive reply that is brief and nondefensive. Bank Image Objections must be overcome if market penetration is to be increased and perceptions or misperceptions are to be changed.

Turnover Objection

The Turnover Objection, "You are my fourth account officer in the last ten months," is an objection that many bankers face daily. Reorganizations, promotions, retirements, pirating, and career changes result in what seems to be excessive turnover among bankers. This kind of objection is best handled before it occurs. The transition should be made smoothly and professionally by the present banker or by a manager. Ideally a personal introduction should be made, and when that is not possible, the manager should telephone the customer to discuss the change and promote the capabilities of the new account officer. The new officer should be completely debriefed on the new account and be prepared to demonstrate relationship stability by discussing the tenure of his or her manager, the industry focus, the team approach, their own commitment to the relationship, their experience, and so on. They should also inquire about specific inconveniences incurred by the customer because of the changes. For example, bankers might say, "I studied your file and apologize for the changes that have occurred. May I ask whether there has been a specific problem due to this? . . . Prior to the meeting, I met with . . . to become familiar with. . . . Our team approach. . . . " When there is ongoing turnover, managers should stress their management overview role to the customer. If turnover is excessive, management should review its selection process, reward structure, training, and organizational system to idenfity possible contributing factors. A stable sales force is very important in effective relationship management.

Insurmountable Objections

Insurmountable objections are just that! In spite of the Objection Response Model, product knowledge, or the Total Offer, some objections *cannot be offset.* When bankers probe, gain an understanding of the nature of the objection, and address it, they sometimes find that the objection cannot be overcome. For example, a customer may require information at 8:30 A.M., and the bank's Balance Reporting may not be able to deliver it until 9:00 A.M. Bankers should recognize the paramount weight of the particular objection and be prepared to shift gears. If they cannot do so, the interview may be terminated. Recognizing insurmountable objections requires judgment. Bankers should respond to insurmountable objections by acknowledging them. Bankers should be the ones to say, "From what we have discussed, it looks as if this may not be the product [deal] for you at this time." This requires courage, but recognizing and facing such objections do in fact save time and build credibility. They can have the additional benefit of uncovering smoke-screen objections or finding new opportunities. In concluding a topic or an interview, bankers should remember the often-repeated saying: "Never burn bridges."

Premature Objections

Sometimes a customer will raise an objection too early in the sales interview for bankers to handle it adequately. Bankers must be prepared to recognize this when it happens and say they would like to address it but would appreciate it if particular point could be delayed for a few minutes. Evaluating the readiness to discuss a particular objection is a part of controlling the sales call, and bankers should remember that they do not have to respond to an objection or question immediately. They can acknowledge the objection and suggest that it be covered a little later. Bankers should of course remember to address the point that was shelved later in the interview. Pacing objections is quite different from attempting to avoid them. Objections must be faced and even *unearthed* by bankers, since objectons that are dodged are liekly to reappear as major barriers later in the sale.

Manipulative Objections

Although many objections are genuine, bankers should be prepared for objections that are used by customers to *manipulate the situation*. There are a number of pressure objections, such as better offers, other opportunities, threats to pull the account, being overbanked, and others. Pressure objections can be obvious, such as ''We'll pull our account,'' or ''I want to speak with your manager,'' or subtle, such as ''I need a decision now because I'm going on vacation,'' or ''All the other banks agree.'' By asking for specifics, bankers can show their concern, gather specific information, and *test the authenticity of the objection.*

The predominant attitude of the pressure strategy objection is ''take it or leave it.'' Bankers should be prepared to test the waters if they don't want to fold under the weight of a ploy. The Objection Response Model is very helpful in withstanding and overcoming pressure objections. Open-ended questions that require the customer to back up, explain, or further define what he or she has said are the best tools that bankers have to counteract a manipulative customer. Bankers should use these tools coupled with their judgment and experience in handling this kind of customer and establishing a working relationship.

Objections Bankers Can't Answer Immediately

There are basically three situations in which bankers should not attempt to answer an objection (or a question):

1 When they don't know the answer.
2 When although they know the answer, the marketing strategy for the product (because of the options, complexity, or sliding scale for the pricing) requires that the specialist be called in to discuss technical questions or objections.
3 When by answering the objection they risk making a premature commitment.

If an objection is raised for which bankers do not know the answer, they should *admit* that they do not have the details, state that they will research the information, and, of course, report back to the customer. Bankers should not be defensive or apologetic. They could also ask what prompts the question to gain insight into the customer's concern or interest. Not having a particular answer can often be used by bankers to their advantage, because it creates the perfect opportunity to arrange an appointment for a specialist. However, overreliance on specialists cannot substitute for preparation. To recognize opportunities and to develop them, bankers should know the basics of the products marketed in their area.

When an objection or question is raised that requires input from specialists, bankers should use the objection as an opportunity to gather information for the specialists, so that the joint call can be more fruitful. For the wide range of products that require technical assistance, a joint call *with* the specialists is appropriate. If bankers cannot give specific pricing because the price is negotiable or a study is required, bankers basically should defer the price to the specialists. Price objections on noncredit products, as well as questions that require technical expertise, analysis, or negotiation, should be deferred to the specialists.

An example of making a referral to the specialists for Direct Deposit payroll is:

Customer.   I think we'll lose our float.

Banker.   That's an important consideration. When do your employees cash their checks?

Customer.   Within a few days—some in three or four days.

Banker.   In companies like yours, we have found that the reduction in check processing costs . . . usually more than offsets the reduction in float. What are your thoughts on having me arrange an appointment with Tim Jones, our cash management specialist, who can review your specific situation and give you some projections . . . ?

Customer.   Fine. I'd like to look hard at what it will mean to us.

Banker.   Let's set the appointment for later this week. Would Thursday morning . . . ? Also it would be helpful if I could get some preliminary information so Tim can prepare for the call. You have 500 employees; from whom can I get . . . ?

Bankers can also delay answering an objection in situations in which they are not prepared to commit themselves. They can say that they'd like to take a certain subject back and review the options, give it more thought, or confer with colleagues. For example, in discussing Foreign Exchange:

Customer.   Can't I use my present line?

Banker.   I understand your interest in that. However, to ensure that you have use of that line for your . . . , we will open a Foreign Exchange line for you.

Customer.   For how much? Can you give me X dollars?

Banker.   Let me make note of that. I'd like to take this back and ensure that we extend to you the maximum line that reflects our relationship with you. I'll be in touch with you on. . . .

Deferring the answer to an objection to another meeting or a later date can be a helpful sales strategy. Deferring objections is totally different from avoiding objections. In the long run, objections cannot be avoided or circumvented, since they are likely to reappear and block the sale at a later time. But deferring objections can give bankers the opportunity to plan a strategy that will satisfy the customer and protect the interests of the bank.

Customers Who Don't Object

Objections can take many forms. They can be blatant criticisms and complaints; they can come in the form of questions; they can be delivered sarcastically or humorously; they can be spoken without a word, with a raise of an eyebrow, a tilt of the head, or a rub of the nose indicating rejection or annoyance. But what does it mean when no objections are raised? A sales interview without objections often signals trouble. It can indicate courtesy—or boredom. Objections at the very least reflect customer attention and appraisal. They also provide bankers with valuable insight into the customer's thinking.

Bankers should *welcome* objections as opportunities to sell the merits of their products relative to customer needs. They are so important that bankers should ferret them out. When objections are not forthcoming, bankers should test the customer by asking some questions aimed at uncovering concerns and reservations. If a customer does not raise an objection that experience says should be asked, bankers should use questions to stimulate the objections and encourage the customer to express his or her reservations.

Particularly if bankers think there is an objection that could block the sale at a later time, they should raise the point in a nonthreatening manner. For example, in selling a Trust Service, it may be appropriate for bankers to ask, "What are your thoughts on having your *attorney* join us for our next meeting?" Since the attorney may be a key figure later, bankers can gain information concerning the attorney's role and create the opportunity to develop a relationship with the attorney. Objections that will be stumbling blocks later should be raised by the banker as a way to propel the sale forward. Unearthing and exploring important objections do not increase problems, but rather prevent them.

Summary of Fielding Objections

The key elements of a sale are employed in fielding objections. Bankers actually orchestrate minisales each time they respond to an objection. The opening (repeating the objection), probing questions (clarifying the objection), Motivation Lever (identifying the customer's concerns), product knowledge (Total Offer of features linked with benefits to satisfy the objection), and the incremental close (checking for agreement) are all utilized in satisfying objections. Perhaps the secrets to fielding objections are: to allow for customer input; to refrain from giving product information until customers have had an opportunity to disclose what they really want and need to know to make a decision with confidence; and to respond in a positive rather than adversarial manner.

Bankers should use the Objection Response Model to communicate their product information. By developing the dialogue as they answer objections, bankers are in a better position to make certain that they are responding to and *satisfying* what is on the customer's mind. Customers who are encouraged to express their concerns and who are asked for their feedback concerning their satisfaction with bankers' replies are often more receptive to accepting new or unfamiliar information.

It is not usually the inherent *differences* among products or systems that cause a customer to choose one banker over another, but rather it is bankers' ability to *communicate* the differences or *explain* the similarities relative to the customer's situation that distinguishes one bank, one product, or one banker from another. Product knowledge is of course essential if bankers are to overcome objections, but product knowledge alone is not enough. Bankers may have a great deal of product knowledge, but unless they can consultatively communicate it, they may be unable to convert customer resistance into customer confidence with the information that they provide. Objections must be answered in a way that keeps communications open so that bankers and their ideas can keep coming back. Product knowledge combined with the Objection Response Model increases bankers' ability to convert objections into selling points and helps them advance in the sale.

Incremental Close

Checking for Understanding and Agreement

Unlike the idea of the traditional closing in which the banker asks for the order at the end of a *sales presentation*, the incremental close is used *throughout a sales interview*. By using probing questions incrementally to determine whether the customer agrees with and accepts the information that is presented, bankers can check for agreement and understanding, gain insight into the customer's reactions, evaluate their own effectiveness, and determine the appropriate next step.

By contrast with the traditional close that occurs at the conclusion of the sales presentation, or the trial close that begins midway, the incremental close is used during every important part of the sale as a way to solicit customer feedback. Checking for agreement and understanding every time an important point is covered can eliminate the painful sting that many bankers associate with the traditional close, since they will have an indication of what the customer's decision will be based on his or her feedback.

Bankers can nail down points of agreement and address obstacles *as they surface*, rather than letting them accumulate until the end of the sale. By involving the customer throughout the sale, bankers are less likely to be surprised at the end of the interview since they are likely to have probably achieved closure on the major points discussed. Incremental closing enables bankers to adjust their approach to the customer based on his or her direct feedback. Bankers can also use the incremental close to guide and pace the discussion and prevent unproductive and unwarranted jumps from topic to topic without ever achieving closure.

The incremental close assists bankers in building agreement, identifying points of disagreement, determining their positions, focusing on customer concerns, and helping them *predict* the customer's readiness to buy. Using the information provided by the customer, bankers can estimate the appropriateness of asking for the order. Incremental closing creates an environment in which bankers can be in sync with their customers, and the final arrangements are not a separate event but rather the *action step* in a series of incremental closings.

Using Probing Questions

Probing questions are the basic tools of the incremental close; incremental summaries can also be used in conjunction with probing questions, but since it is what the customer says that is most important, probing questions should be used as the primary tool for closing incrementally. By using probing questions to test for understanding and agreement throughout the interview, bankers are able to appraise their progress, confirm points of agreement, and clarify points of disagreement so that they can move forward in the sale. The customer's responses will reveal areas of discord and harmony and will help bankers determine whether to proceed, backtrack, probe, or redirect the sales interview. Incremental closings should be used after a key feature and benefits are presented after the customer's questions and objections have been answered. By asking such open-ended questions as "How would . . . contribute to your pool of management information?" or "What are your thoughts on this?" bankers can better estimate their effectiveness *during* the sales call and make the necessary adjustments to respond to the customer's thoughts and needs. Also, by summarizing briefly during the interview, bankers can advance in the sale and increase the likelihood that the customer is with them and that they are with the customer. Many bankers state that they would like to be able to "read" their customers. Although body language is extremely important, the incremental close provides a direct and objective way to understand what is going on in the customer's mind relative to the sales call. By using probing questions to close incrementally, bankers can build an on going feedback system into their sales interviews.

Reducing Rejection

Bankers who do not close incrementally may find themselves without the order at the end of the sales call, without knowing what went wrong. Reluctance to close often stems from a desire to avoid rejection. Unfortunately, this ostrich thinking results in wasted time and wasted effort and does not alter the negative responses that the customer may have. On the contrary, being aware of a customer's resistance from incremental feedback can provide bankers with the opportunity to satisfy the resistance. Bankers should be aware of how they are doing so that they can evaluate their selling effectiveness, identify lack of customer interest or customer concern, make strategy decisions, flexibly adjust their strategy to meet customer needs, and determine the customer's readiness to move into the action step. There is no better way to do this than by using the incremental close.

In practice, the incremental close should be used by bankers as a way to close successfully. By using the incremental close to check for understanding and agreement throughout the sales interview, bankers can reduce the situtations in which the customer rejects the action step. It will also help bankers avoid premature closing before the customer is sold or before the customer has confidence in the value of the product to him or her. Sometimes bankers rush asking for the business because they do not have the product information or the selling skills to sustain the discussion. It will also help them avoid lengthy monologue discussions in which they have no way of knowing how the customer is responding. When the close is rejected they usually do not know where they lost their customers and therefore cannot address specific parts of the sale that need mending.

When an incremental close meets with a negative response from a customer, bankers are at least aware that there is dissatisfaction, misunderstanding, or a lack of interest in a particular area, feature, or benefit. They can probe, reexplain, redirect, or introduce new information. The incremental close does not come with a 100% guarantee, but it does increase the banker's ability to *predict* the customer's responsiveness based on the direct feedback provided by the customer.

To meet the competitive pressures in the banking industry, bankers are being told to "ask for the business." Unfortunately, they often ask for the business before the product's features and benefits are understood by the customer relative to his or her needs and interests. Although asking for business is a must, it is more important to *get* it. Therefore, when the feedback from the incremental close is overwhelmingly negative, bankers should *not* ask for the business. The banker should be the one who says, "This does not look like the product or deal for you at this point." This may seem radical or suicidal, but if indeed the product is not right for the customer and he or she recognizes it, bankers can demonstrate their professional judgment, maintain control of the sales call, and save time by also recognizing the inevitable. *When consulting with customers, it should be the banker, not the customer, who suggests that a product may not be appropriate.* Feedback from the incremental close will enable the banker to do this. Used this way, the incremental close can save valuable time, save face, and in many instances assist bankers in saving sales that appear to be lost, by unearthing hidden objections or hidden agendas and reopening the discussion based on new issues or information.

Bankers always need to apply common sense and judgment in estimating the customer's readiness and responsiveness to buy. In the face of customer resistance, bankers should try to satisfy the resistance *before* they try to close. Closing incrementally can help the banker increase sales by checking throughout the sale for the customer's acceptance, rather than waiting until the end of the sale when a *number* of negatives, questions, or concerns may have been built up in the customer's mind, blocking the sale. The incremental close keeps bankers in touch with customer reactions and increases their sensitivity to points of their deals that have to be modified or offset. They also assist bankers in tallying up their areas of strength and deciding when to go for their action step.

Some examples of incremental closings are:

General.   What are your thoughts on this? How does that sound?

Specific.   What are your thoughts on reducing clerical costs and freeing up your staff? How might our automatic tracing help with the problem of uncollected funds?

Summary

The incremental close helps bankers estimate the extent to which they have succeeded in communicating their product's value relative to the customer's needs. It alerts them to the next appropriate step: whether to continue, review a particular area, probe, conclude the interview, proceed in the sale, or implement the action step.

There are seven major benefits of the incremental close:

1 It improves communication between bankers and customers.
2 It increases the likelihood that bankers and customers are in sync and stay that way throughout the sale.
3 It increases bankers' *flexibility* in adjusting their sales approach, product emphasis, content, and pacing.
4 It provides bankers with a position of strength from which they can initiate appropriate action steps.

5 It unearths problems, concerns, and misunderstandings and provides an opportunity to correct them.

6 It fosters a dialogue.

7 It reduces rejection when an action step is suggested.

The Action Step

The First Step of Implementation

The objective of the incremental close is to lead to a positive *action step*. The action step is the final part of the incremental close and the first step in implementing the sale. The action step flows from positive incremental closings. It can be initiated by the banker or by the customer. Often when bankers properly exercise the incremental close, *it is the customer* who initiates the action step by asking, "How do I get started?" If the customer does not initiate the action step, bankers should summarize key benefits and suggest the first step of the implementation. For example: "When would it be convenient to meet with our cash management specialists to discuss your specific requirements so that you can have timely access to your international balances and reduce idle balances?"

Determining Action Steps

Depending on the complexity of the product, the procedures and internal systems, or the size of the bank, the action step for a particular product can include securing a financial statement or other pertinent data, making an appointment with a specialist who will complete the sale, or completing the sale (by finalizing arrangements and signing necessary documents, beginning the implementation of the product, and proceeding with installation).

Since action steps differ from product to product, bankers should have a clear understanding of the appropriate action step for each product and should plan possible action steps before each sales call. For example, a banker's sales call objectives may be to qualify and interest the prospect, gather data such as a schedule of receivables, and set up an appointment for the international specialists. The action step should emanate from the sales call objective.

In initiating the action step, bankers should be alert to closing signals from the customers, such as comments concerning cost, requests for specific information, requests for start-up time, alertness in facial expression, and body language such as closing a pen. Closing signals should not be ignored or they can cost the sale. As they initiate the action step, bankers should summarize key features and benefits and points of agreement.

There are various closing techniques, such as the minor point close ("Would Tuesday or Wednesday be more convenient?"), the balance sheet close ("Let's compare the total offers to you," or "Let's look at how that would affect your cash flow," using a sheet of paper with a line drawn down the center), and others. Bankers should not look at closing as an event that takes place at the end of a sale, however. The keys to effective closing are recognizing the need to begin incremental closings early in the sale and having a specific action step in mind before the sales call begins.

To facilitate decisions and accelerate implementation, bankers should conclude every sales call with an action step. The action step is designed to reduce the number of "hello calls." Action steps should define the *next step*. They should be specific as to concluding arrangements, time and purpose, and participants of the next appointment or next step. *The action step should not be left in the customer's control* or in the customer's court. Bankers must take the responsibility for setting the time, place, and participants of the next meeting *before concluding the interview*. In situations in which a bank specialist or other bank colleagues must be involved, bankers should assume the responsibility of getting back to the customer and making the final arrangements. Whenever possible bankers should participate in the next meeting with the specialists and customers.

Contradictory Messages

When customers, contrary to their own positive responses during the incremental closings, reject the action step, bankers should try to uncover the reason for the apparent discrepancy. Unless the customer was insincere in responding positively to the incremental closing, bankers should have anticipated the customer's negative response and should not have initiated the action step. Either the customer was insincere in his or her feedback, or the banker did not use the incremental close as effectively as he or she might have. As much for their own development as to recover the sale, bankers should politely ask the customer why it seemed that he or she had agreed with X,Y, and Z and then had decided against the product. This can reveal information that can reopen the sale. If the sale cannot be recovered at the time, bankers should conclude the meeting in a positive and professional manner, always leaving the door open. Whenever possible, bankers should not conclude the interview unless they are satisfied that the objections have been unearthed and discussed and the *Total Offer* has been presented, reviewed, and understood, even if it is not accepted.

Summary

The incremental close and the action step work together. The incremental close is the traffic light of the sale, indicating to bankers when to stop, when to pause, and when to move ahead. It provides bankers with a way to get direct customer feedback throughout the sales call and signals to bankers when action steps are appropriate. Positive incremental closings usually lead to positive action steps. The action step is the first step in completing, implementing, or installing the product or service. It sets implementation in motion and accelerates bringing in new business.

Body Signals

Nonverbal Messages

The body communicates with every gesture. Crossing or uncrossing the legs, raising an eyebrow, folding or unfolding the arms, putting on or removing glasses—all these are ways in which a customer unintentionally and genuinely communicates his or her reactions or thoughts.

Customers continuously send out a host of body signals, both positive and negative. Bankers who are aware of them are in an excellent position to use the nonverbal cues to their advantage. Before looking at some specific body signals that can be transmitted in a selling situation, it is important to recognize that there is no universal translation for body signals. Individual differences, cultural differences, and circumstances can influence body language, and bankers should exercise caution in interpreting it, if they are to avoid making generalizations and assumptions that can be costly. But certain gestures do in practice consistently convey particular messages. The following signals and interpretations are examples of gestures that occur frequently during sales interviews.

Body Signals	Possible Sales Implications
Clasping hands behind head, elbows out.	Disengaging. The meeting is over, for all intents and purposes.
Putting glasses on.	The interesting part has begun.
Removing glasses.	Disagreement (don't see eye to eye).
Leaning forward.	Interested and involved.
Backing away.	Retreating; touched a sore point.
Making eye contact.	Attention.
Folding arms across chest tightly.	Guarded, negative, threatened, rejecting.
Rubbing nose.	Mild or strong *negative* reaction.
Tapping.	Impatience, nervousness.
Doodling.	Not interested; wants the topic to be more relevant to his or her needs.
Breaking eye contact and quickly glancing down.	Listener wants to talk.
Closing book, closing pen, moving materials.	Overstay of welcome.
Joining hands, fingers touching in steeple fashion.	Superior, pontificating. (I am accomplished and expert in this area.)
Crossing legs in toward salesperson.	Positive rapport.
Crossing legs away from salesperson.	Something is wrong; there may be a need to change approach.
Pushing chair away from banker.	Negative and backing away from the deal.
Moving chair in toward banker.	Interested, involved, and positive.
Customer's choice of chair.	Open, supportive (right angle) or adversarial, combative (directly across).

These are a few of the many body gestures that can be exhibited during the sales interview. All people, of course, utilize body language as a natural and what appears to be an instinctive part of their communications system. By reading and using body language, bankers can increase their understanding of their customers and therefore increase their sales effectiveness.

The first step in understanding body language is to become aware of the role of gestures in communication. Once bankers recognize a body signal, they can decide how to interpret it and what response, if any, to make. Bankers should be careful in ascribing meaning to particular body signals and should keep in mind that a particular gesture may in fact be signaling a negative or positive reaction of the customer toward the banker, or that it may be coincidental and have nothing to do with the sales interview or the banker. Bankers can test the message by tactfully asking a question, restating the concern, or finessing a comment to observe the customer's reaction. If it appears that the gesture signaled a negative reaction, bankers should tread gently and make the necessary adjustments to regain ground and to make the customer more comfortable. Bankers who are trying to achieve agreement should modify their type of questions or the point of view or perspective being developed as a way to build or reestablish rapport. The objective of the modification is not to manipulate the customer but rather to reopen the channels of communications.

Bankers should be aware that body signals occur constantly during the sales interview. They are delivered through facial expression, body gestures, glances, and posture. They can accompany verbal language or can be delivered when no sound is heard. Body signals are often transmitted before a single word is spoken.

By taking the time to observe them, making the necessary adjustment to capitalize on positive signals, and initiating a different approach to minimize or eliminate the negative ones, bankers can increase their effectiveness.

The following is an example of using a body signal during a sales interview to *supplement verbal messages:*

Situation	Body Signal	Possible Sales Implication	Banker's Response	Result
Banker is seated in customer's conversation area. Banker is on chair and customer is on sofa at a right angle. Banker makes a comment or asks a question and customer crosses leg away from banker and rubs nose.	Crossing leg away from banker and rubbing nose.	May signal that customer is becoming defensive. Generally these are negative signals.	Banker should soften or rephrase what he or she said, ask a non-threatening question (one the customer can positively answer), or give a supportive comment.	Customer's defensiveness should be reduced; legs will probably be uncrossed, or cross in toward the banker.

Of course, body signals should be evaluated in conjunction with verbal messages. Sometimes they support the verbal message and sometimes they contradict it. Bankers should use their judgment in choosing which message to respond to. Missing body signals can be as much of a problem as misreading them, and bankers should apply both judgment and experience in reading signals to use them to their advantage.

Summary

Since body signals can give insight into what interests, bores, pleases, or threatens customers, they are important in sales. They should be used with the other key elements, especially the incremental close, which provides direct verbal feedback to communicate more effectively with customers. As important as the customer's body signals are to the banker, the banker's body signals are often more important. The whole concept of first impression relates to body signals. The manner of entering an office gives clues to attitude, confidence, experience, and rank. Bankers should be conscious of their own body signals and should communicate attention and interest in their eye contact and body posture. Understanding body signals requires alertness, observation, and sensitivity—three qualities necessary in consulting with customers. Body signals should be used to supplement the verbal messages communicated by the customer.

The Sales Environment

The Setting for the Sale

The sales environment—the place and time in which the sales interview is held—is a peripheral but important element of the sale. Because of the nature of the seller–customer relationship, it is usually the banker who initiates the call and who travels to the customer's office or site. Some facilities that are provided by customers are conducive to a sales interview, and some are less than ideal. In a private and comfortable setting, bankers can more easily get the attention of the customer; the challenge becomes much greater in offices or sites that are hotbeds of activity filled with ringing telephones, stoppers-by, and all the other factors that disrupt and interfere with the sales interview.

Since bankers are the ones who are calling, they usually have little control over the kind of setting they will find. There are, however, certain things that they can do to control the environment they are given, so that they can maximize the time they spend with their customers. The following aspects of the environment affect the call and can have a positive influence on the sales call when they are understood.

The Office

Bankers can take sales cues from the environment, particularly the customer's office. Offices are designed in a variety of ways. They may be bare, crowded with pictures, disorganized, functional, or elegant. Many customers have the bare essentials—a desk arrangement and perhaps a separate conversation area—and some have elaborate settings. Regardless of the kind of office, bankers should keep their eyes open and observe and utilize it to their advantage.

Bankers should be alert to the setup of the office. The office itself can provide the topic for rapport buildup, and if it is the customer's own office (beware: it might not be) it can give insight into the customer's interests or approach. An example is the case of the customer with a book on expensive foreign cars on his desk. The customer spoke enthusiastically about his new car with the banker for about ten minutes. Later in the call, when the banker discussed the stock transfer system, he tied in "finest quality" and "image to the stockholders" in a positive and constructive way. An office often reveals something that the banker can use to understand the customer and satisfy his or her requirements.

No Office

For many middle-market bankers or bankers who visit on site, customer offices or at least private offices with closed doors are a rare luxury. Bankers often find themselves meeting with their customers standing up amid an active business environment in which the customer is involved. This situation is most difficult, and on the whole consultative selling cannot consistently take place in such an environment.

Identifying needs and discussing products require the attention and focus of the banker and the customer. Trying to conduct a sales interview amid interruptions and distractions can be disturbing and unsettling, and it usually proves unproductive. There is no solution to this problem except to use the active environment to gather basic information, ask some probing questions, identify possible needs, show concern, and set a time to meet when there is less activity—after five, before nine-thirty, for lunch or dinner, or at the bank, to see a particular operations area or attend a luncheon. In general, bankers (in a sales role) should visit the customer because it is usually more convenient for the customer. In situations in which the customer's environment repeatedly proves to be distracting to the sales interview, it is advisable to remove the customer from the environment or to reset an appointment for a time that is more convenient and less distracting for the customer and the bankers.

Office Seating

Most often bankers are offered a seat *across* the desk from the customer. This is perfectly acceptable and should be graciously accepted. Although it is the most common office arrangement, it is the least desirable for the seller. It presents several significant sales problems. First, the desk can be a barrier separating the banker from the customer; second, a subordination role can be implied; and, third, it establishes a "lock-horns" or adversary position. Bankers cannot do anything to change the seating arrangement short of moving furniture, which is of course (usually) unacceptable. One top negotiator, when given a lock-horns opposite seat, moves it an inch or two as he sits down to throw off the adversary arrangement, unless it is his aim to lock horns. Similarly, a photo recently printed in The *New York Times* showed two world leaders with their backs to the camera, moving heavy arm chairs to create an advocate right-angle arrangement and eliminate the lock-horns seating arrangement.

So too should bankers be conscious of the seating arrangement and attempt to use it to their benefit. Some customers have a choice of chairs near their desks. Bankers should wait for a signal from the customer indicating where to sit, but should move toward the *right-angle* seating whenever it is an option. Right-angle seating is conducive to consultative sales since it represents an advocate relationship. When there is a seating arrangement around a coffee table, bankers should also try to avoid a lock-horns arrangement. They must think quickly and select seats that will complement (not oppose) the place in which their customer is sitting or is apt to sit.

Continuous Interruptions

When there is a continuous stream of interruptions—telephone calls, questions, problem solving, miniconsultations, stoppers-by—it is virtually impossible to consult with the customer. During a sales call plagued with interruptions, bankers should be patient and understanding and should not show annoyance or indignation or take the confusion or possible rudeness personally. The customer expects the banker to be sympathetic to how busy he or she is. If the interruptions do not stop, bankers should supportively acknowledge the busy schedule and *suggest that a new time be set that would be more convenient for the customer and more conducive to discussing the customer's situation, requirements, and opportunities.* Bankers should use their present appointment as an opportunity to set the next interview, perhaps to be held at a restaurant or at the bank or during off-business hours.

Time

In a broad definition, the time allocated for the meeting is also a part of the selling environment. Bankers should have an idea of the amount of time that they will have with the customer and should prepare accordingly. If the time that had been set for the meeting is cut short, bankers should resist the temptation to try to fit one hour's worth of discussion into 15 minutes. When meetings are shortened bankers should gather some preliminary information and use their time to interest the customer in the next full interview.

As for the best time to have meetings, morning hours before lunch are generally optimal times; however, bankers should avoid the "not a good time" syndrome that puts off meetings because it's Monday, Friday, after lunch, too late in the day, too early, near a holiday, and so on. Although judgment must be used in scheduling sales time, and some days (such as July 3 if it falls on a Monday) may not be the best time, all business and many nonbusiness hours are prime time for selling.

Summary of the Ten Elements of a Sale

By understanding the ten elements of a sale, bankers can prepare for and conduct productive sales calls on a more consistent basis. Many bankers are seeking ways to maximize the time they spend with their customers. They are seeking assistance in making more effective sales calls. The sales call is really the manifestation of the precall planning. A major factor in the success of a sales call is the *preparation* of the ten elements. Bankers should prepare for each element prior to making a call. Whether the call is a prospect (first) sales call, or a sales call with an established customer, bankers should set a call objective and flexibly utilize the ten elements to achieve their sales objective. Whether the objective of the call is general, such as establishing rapport, identifying needs, learning about the customer's situation, or recognizing possible opportunities for the bank, or more targeted, such as establishing a need for international services and introducing the bank's international capabilities, the ten elements should be used.

The ten elements should be a part of all sales calls with prospects and customers alike. Of course the nature of the relationship will influence the depth of each element. Prospect calls will focus primarily on establishing rapport and identifying needs through the opening, Motivation Lever, and probing questions. However, unless objections are fielded successfully, incremental closings are applied periodically, and appropriate features and benefits are discussed, there may not be a second call. A corporate treasurer boasts, "I will see any banker *once*." And unless an action step (the next step) is determined, the call may become another "hello call" with minimal potential for new business. So too, calls with established customers must utilize all of the ten elements, with the appropriate emphasis on each element.

Although sales calls with existing customers are often more focused in their objective, and, based on their knowledge of the customer and previous calls, bankers have preselected a product or product family to explore, they should avoid falling into the trap of introducing the product without first establishing need and interest (Motivation Lever) on the part of the customer. When assumed needs do not exist, bankers should be prepared to switch gears. Probing questions will help establish genuine needs.

Using the ten elements during *all* sales calls will assist bankers in achieving their objectives. The time frame, pacing, and sequence of the elements will of course vary according to each customer and customer relationship, but the elements should be a constant factor in all sales interviews if consultative selling is to be achieved. It is through the preparation of the ten elements that bankers can *control* the sales call. The customers are the variables, and the ten elements of a sale are the constants. Bankers should approach each sale as professionals who know what they are doing. Of course, they should be prepared to jockey the elements to meet the customer's style, but they should not lose track or control of where they are in the sale. The banker's skill in using the ten elements provides a way to maximize control.

Bankers' sales calls should be organized in that they should use the ten elements as a flexible framework for each sale. The ten key elements provide a process, *not* a script. They are an invisible vehicle for communicating information in an individualized and complete way. The ten elements are helpful in developing a consultative sales environment. They provide a transferable system that bankers can use to discuss any product or deal. Although products, customers, and bankers are different, the underlying sales–communication process for a consultative interview is always the same. The ten elements are not sequential. They are parallel skills that bankers can draw on before, during, and after sales calls to improve their sales effectiveness.

It often is the individual banker who distinguishes one bank or one product from another, and bankers who utilize the consultative selling approach can orchestrate effective and successful sales interviews with a wide range of customers. The ten elements are important in effective consultative sales calls. With the exception of the opening, Motivation Lever, and action step, the sequence of the elements is completely irrelevant. Bankers must juggle the elements to help the customer sell himself or herself. Consultative selling is almost "selling without selling," since the focus of the sale is the customer's needs and not the product. Many bankers and others in sales expect selling to be a tug of war between buyer and seller. The tug-of-war approach to sales is an approach that is devoid of Motivation Levers and a customer-driven sales dialogue. The consultative approach to sales works particularly well for bankers because their aim is to develop long-term, mutually beneficial relationships between customers and the bank, which are based on trust and satisfaction. The ten elements are the tools for building such relationships.

PREPARING FOR THE SALES CALL

Preparation is a major factor in making effective sales calls and in maximizing sales opportunities. Whether it is a sales call on a prospective customer or a current customer, bankers are required to do their homework if they want to maximize their sales results.

As bankers plan for their sales calls, they should focus on:

1 Understanding the products that are to be marketed in their area.
2 Developing accurate customer knowledge and identifying customer needs.
3 Developing sales plans *before* each sales interview.

Outline of the Sales Call

Prior to making the actual sales call, bankers should outline their sales objectives and activities. The outline of the sales call (written or mental) is designed to help bankers maintain control during the sales interview by avoiding surprises. Outlining the sales call also enables bankers to build *flexibility* into the sales plan.

The outline should include the following:

The objective of the sales call

Anticipated needs

The approach to open the call

Probing questions to qualify the customer

Probing questions to identify needs or problems (product opportunities) and to create an awareness of needs

The banker's own strengths and weaknesses and the customer's assumed strengths and weaknesses

Knowledge of products that seem appropriate for the customer, at least tentatively

Tentative priority of features and benefits to be discussed

Representative customer in similar industry

Anticipated objections and responses

Competitive information

Action steps

Many bankers state that they need assistance with their sales presentation. Rarely do they request assistance with their planning for sales calls. Not appreciating the direct relationship between sales call planning and sales results can be a problem. Much of what takes place during the sale should be déja vu for the bankers. They should have defined their objective, prepared their opening, organized their questions, anticipated the objections, and made assumptions about customer needs. The sales call should be new, fresh, spontaneous, and organized from the customer's perspective, but the essential elements of it *should not be new to bankers*. The sales call should be a reflection of the flexible plan they developed prior to the call. Effective selling is the result of effective preparation and call planning. Bankers should be prepared for their part of the sales call and should orchestrate the call to make it a productive use of time for both parties.

Although bankers consciously distinguish between planning the sales call and what actually takes place during the sales call, they often fail to recognize the direct relationship between the two. Observation and analysis of more than 1000 sales calls reveal that many bankers expect the call to develop simply by virtue of the fact that banker and customer are together. In discussing planning, many bankers express their belief that "you have to wait until you meet with the customer." This is at best one-quarter true, and it dangerously borders on "flying by the seat of your pants." Certainly the customer's needs, situation, and intentions are key factors in determining what is finally accomplished in the sales call, but that does substitute for the need to be thoroughly prepared with the ten elements for several possible sales discussions before entering the customer's office. The onus is on the banker to set the stage and guide the sales agenda. If the customer has a strong grip on his or her needs, options, and plans, the banker's orchestration becomes less difficult, but bankers should never relinquish their responsibilities in hopes that the customer is prepared!

Exhibit 2 is a planner that can be adapted by bankers in preparing for their sales calls.

Exhibit 2 Sample Sales Call Planner

Relationship Name: _____ Banker: _____

Key Contact(s)/Titles: _____ Date of Call: _____

—Face to Face—Telephone

Sales Objective(s)

Customer's Assumed Motivation Lever	Decision Makers	Present Operating Mode

Product(s) to Discuss

Sales Strategy
Opening

Probing Questions	Qualifying Criteria

Features	Benefits

Anticipated Objections	Resolution

Active Competition

Internal Planning/Joint Call	Sales Environment/Materials

Action Step

Comments

DECLINING À TRANSACTION

Although considerable emphasis is placed on encouraging the customer to say yes, sometimes bankers find it necessary to decline. Declining without damaging the relationship is the ultimate sales challenge.

Bankers should be sensitive to the impact declining can have on the relationship or the customer's attitude toward the bank. Every possible effort should be made not to "burn bridges." The ideal way to decline a transaction, of course, is to get the customer to say no to the transaction himself or herself. This takes an investment of time and even then may not be possible. A comment such as "We'd be happy to consider this, but have you thought through . . . ?" can assist the customer in evaluating the prudence of the transaction for his or her situation and seeing why it is not advisable. Tips for keeping the door open include: (first and foremost) knowing the *reason* for saying no to the transaction or relationship; explaining the reason in a clear, nondefensive manner; saying no to the transaction rather than to the person (using the word *this* rather than *you*); showing empathy; and suggesting alternatives whenever possible. Bankers should not procrastinate over declining since a prolonged delay can be just as upsetting to customers as the decline itself, or even more so, since it may prevent them from arranging for an alternative, block opportunities for getting refunds, and so on. Customers often read "no news" as "good news"; therefore, it is important to get back to customers quickly.

When bankers do not know the specific reason, it is essential that they ask their managers or credit committee for the detailed information so that they can help the customer understand the reasons for the refusal. Also, whenever possible, bankers should not decline over the telephone. If they must do so, because of time, distance, and/or schedule factors, they should arrange a personal appointment as soon as possible, and set a date and time while they are on the telephone. The objective in declining situations is to retain the relationship or the potential for a future relationship, while declining a particular transaction.

Perhaps the most important rule when declining is to remember that although it may not be possible to satisfy the customer financially, every effort must be made to satisfy the customer emotionally.

JOINT CALLING

Joint calling is an excellent way to bring added value to the customer. Line bankers can call jointly with specialists (product managers, operational, other colleagues with technical expertise), managers, colleagues, and even with a customer or the customer's customer. The primary reasons for joint calling are adding expertise and demonstrating the bank's interest in the customer. Other reasons for joint calling are to assist colleagues (two heads are better than one, balancing the numbers of customers to bankers), develop multilevel contacts in the organization (banker introduces cash manager), use the call as a teaching experience (one junior banker at a time), and increase internal leverage within the bank (customer's name is known in the bank).

To reap the benefits of joint calling, bankers must plan and orchestrate each call. Joint calls that are not planned properly can be fraught with numerous problems, from presenting an uncoordinated impression or disagreeing and arguing in the customer's presence to losing control of the relationship. Some aspects of joint calling that should be taken into consideration as bankers prepare for the call are:

Who is "lead"? (Line bankers should be lead when it is their relationship. Even on calls with seniors, they can retain this if they arrange the call, open, and follow up.)

What background information should be reviewed with team members? (Preparation is key. Contacts, names, information on relationship, needs, problems, etc., should be communicated *prior to* the call.)

What are the roles? (For example: *lead role* discussing credit and addressing relationship problems that might arise and setting the stage for team member; *team role* discussing details of operations, etc.)

What will be said in the introduction? (Introduction of team member, area of bank, expertise, value to be added.)

When and how will transitions be made from line banker to team member or team member to line banker?

How will bankers arrange their seating? (It is usually preferable to integrate customer group and not create "us" against "them" seating.)

Who will take notes? (Taking notes when important information is discussed, do not take notes frantically, and remember to keep eye contact.)

Who will follow up with the customer?

Who will be accountable for initiating the action step, (next step)?

Here are some tips for *preparing* for joint calls:

Clarify roles and expectations before the call.

Agree on objective(s).

Define roles, introductions, sharing of the call.

Share information and discuss background.

Anticipate objections.

Here are some ideas for bankers to remember *during* joint calls:

Do not directly contradict colleague(s) but find a way indirectly to communicate your disagreement if it is crucial. (For example: Junior-level banker says, "We make credit decisions based on the relationship." His team leader could say, "Of course, relationship is key; however, other factors such as . . . are equally. . . .")

Take notes.

Pay attention when customer or *colleague* is talking.

Sit in a place in which signals (glances) can be communicated.

Avoid obvious tactics (good guy, bad guy).

Support team member in comments and body gestures such as nodding agreement.

Listen for key lines (particulary closing lines; then, don't reopen).

Remember that joint calling requires *teamwork*.

Because of the expense of joint calling, it is important that the time and dollars invested be maximized. Sometimes joint calls cannot be made because of geographic or staffing considerations. In situations like these, effective internal communications are essential. Bankers must communicate with their team members prior to and after sales calls if the full resources of the bank are to be used to build multiproduct relationships.

SALES WITH TWO OR MORE CUSTOMERS

Multiple Customers

Frequently bankers are required to meet with several customers at the same time. When this occurs it is usually necessary to modify the ten elements of a sale, since sales meetings with group of customers have additional factors that must be taken into consideration. Whether bankers are to meet with a small group consisting of two or three customers (treasurer, cash manager, and foreign currency manager to discuss a cash management system), or a larger group consisting of eight or more (a board of directors to discuss Investment Management or the employees of a corporation to discuss Direct Depository Payroll), bankers should recognize that group sales calls require special preparation and attention if they are to be effective.

Group sales meetings can be more demanding than one-on-one sales calls. With multiple customers, there are usually multiple Motivation Levers. To compound the situation, there frequently is less opportunity to identify, respond to, and address each customer's need. The dialogue that is the basis of consultative selling on a one-on-one sales interview usually cannot be developed in a large group meeting. To compensate for the increased number of customers and the lack of opportunity for one-on-one exchanges, bankers should approach the ten elements of the sale from a slightly different perspective when the group exceeds ten or so customers. The ten elements should be a part of a sales presentation to a group, but with certain modifications. The following factors should be taken into consideration in modifying the consultative approach.

Multiple Motivation Levers

Since individuals in the group often have different objectives and may have conflicting hidden agendas, bankers should be prepared to recognize and satisfy multiple needs and interests.

A Monologue Format

Because of the increase in the number of customers, there is considerably less opportunity to exchange ideas, identify needs, and actively involve participants during the sales meeting. When the number of customers exceeds ten or so, a consultative *sales interview* (dialogue) becomes difficult, and a consultative *sales presentation* (monologue) may be substituted.

Group Presentation Skills

Communicating with several customers at one time requires an understanding of group communication skills, since each customer expects attention, eye contact, and so on. Regardless of who the decision maker is, bankers should be cognizant of the group and should establish eye contact and give attention and handouts to *all* group members, whether they be family members, subordinates, operations people, or other managers; bankers should also remember to pay appropriate attention to the decision maker.

From Dialogue to Monologue

The most significant difference between a one-on-one sales call and a sales call with a group is the shift from a dialogue to a predominantly monologue format. During a one-on-one sales call, bankers develop a sales interview with customers. In sales calls with a group, bankers are usually required to make presentations. The degree of direct and ongoing interaction distinguishes sales *interviews* from sales *presentations*. The difference, however, does not preclude involvement and interest. Creating and maintaining the involvement and interest of the participants are more challenging in group presentations, since the greater the departure from a dialogue, the more difficult it becomes to capture and keep the attention of the group. Bankers should compensate for the lack of active, ongoing dialogue by taking additional steps in preparing for the meeting and by building an *adaptation* of the ten elements into their presentations. Although presentations to a group are generally more difficult, they do provide bankers with one advantage. Generally the topic of the meeting is decided on prior to the meeting, and bankers are afforded the opportunity to prepare in detail for the predetermined topic.

Preparing for a Group Sales Presentation

Preparation for a sales presentation to a group gains additional importance, since there is often minimal opportunity to develop responses from the customers during the meeting itself. Bankers should research the composition of the audience so that they can be aware of the various orientations and objectives of the members of the group. Before beginning the sales meeting bankers should identify key decision makers as well as the key individuals who will influence the decision. Unless they know their audience, they may approach issues or topics in ways that can threaten, bore, or alienate key individuals in the group if not the entire group.

Yellow-Pad Technique

The most effective way to prepare for a group meeting is for bankers to conduct *individual interviews* with key customers who will be involved in the meeting or at least with the key decision makers *prior* to the group meeting. These individual meetings are referred to as "yellow-pad" meetings because they give bankers the opportunity to take note informally of each customer's needs, interests, and concerns. The notes can be taken mentally or can be recorded, if customer approval is given. Bankers can utilize the yellow-pad data in preparing for their group presentation. These yellow-pad meetings are sometimes thought of as politicking, and in a sense they are. However, it is foolhardy for bankers to meet with a group with little or no idea of the group's modus operandi, orientation, or network. Although they are time-consuming, bankers should take every opportunity to arrange yellow-pad meetings with key individuals if they are interested in maximizing the results of the group meeting.

Yellow-pad meetings not only provide insight into the needs and structure of the individuals in the group but also are instrumental in marshaling support and identifying and reducing obstacles. Such meetings help bankers understand the lay of the land. They are a way for bankers to develop rapport prior to the meeting and to reduce the number of surprises or limit the number and magnitude of unexpected problems that may occur during the group meeting. Of course, the yellow-pad meetings must be conducted on a one-on-one basis or their purpose is defeated, since individuals often are less defensive and more open when they are approached alone. Yellow-pad meetings are the first step in gaining and maintaining control of the group meeting.

When yellow-pad meetings are not possible because of distances, schedules, internal politics, or other factors, bankers should be aware that they may be entering a lion's den. At a very minimum they should use their liaison in the group to find out as much as they can about each of the group members: who will be there, what their roles are, their history with the company, their backgrounds, their relationships with other participants, and their orientation toward the subject to be discussed.

In a consultative way, bankers should gather as much information as they can. A wealth of information, such as irregularities or conflicts of interests, strengths and weaknesses, can be revealed when questions are asked in advance. In questioning the positions of the participants that would be attending one meeting, a banker found out that one of the participants was not an in-house person but rather one of his competitors! Another banker discovered that one of the participants of his meeting was the individual who designed the system that the banker wanted to replace. In the former case, the banker was afforded a tactful way to eliminate the competitor from the audience, and in the latter case a chance to modify his criticism of the present system.

Before meeting with any group, whether it be a few individuals or 20, bankers should have the following information:

What is the objective of the meeting?

What is the topic?

Are the participants aware of the objective and topic?

Who will attend the meeting?

What is the decision-making process?

Who are the decision makers? (Who has the decision-making authority and who can influence the decision?)

What are the background and orientation of each participant?

What are the Motivation Levers of members of the group?

Is the group a mixture of decision makers and users?

Will a colleague from the bank accompany the banker?

Where and when will the meeting be held?

What is the physical setting of the meeting place?

How will the banker use the setting?

Where will the banker sit? Stand?

How much time has been allocated for the meeting?

What materials are needed?

When will questions be asked?

All of the above questions are important in developing the presentation. Unless the orientation of the group is understood, bankers could slant their presentation in a way that reduces its effectiveness. As they prepare for a meeting with several customers they should consider seating arrangements and also the appropriateness of making a joint call.

Seating

The seating arrangements are important in establishing an advocate role. Bankers should strive to sit among a group of 12 to 14 rather than sit at the head of the table or stand apart from the group. Experienced negotiators who are seeking agreement often utilize right-angle or middle-of-the-table seating to develop a positive supportive environment, rather than choosing the head of the table. In selecting their seats around a round, oval, or rectangular table, bankers should avoid positioning themselves head on with the decision maker(s) and should aim for right-angle (non-opposing) seating. Experienced negotiators or salespeople who are already seated in the meeting room while the participants are arriving will whenever possible actually change the seat they initially selected if the decision maker selects an opposing seat. Rising to get coffee or to speak to someone can often provide an opportunity to improve one's seating position.

Developing the Presentation

Based on the data they can gather, bankers should prepare for their presentation. As the group exceeds several participants, dialogue selling is usually inappropriate. But just because a dialogue cannot be developed, bankers should not compromise their effectiveness by making a one-sided, long, boring speech. Bankers should *adapt* the ten elements to ensure that their presentation involves the participants and stimulates a decision to buy.

Adapting the Ten Elements

By utilizing the ten elements in a modified fashion, bankers can ensure participation and maximum involvement.

Opening

The opening, as in a one-on-one sales call, is important. Bankers should consider:

How and by whom will the banker be introduced?

Who will summarize the last meeting or the events that led to the current meeting?

To what extent has the group been properly prepared for the meeting?

How will the banker communicate the objective of the meeting so that it is understood and accepted by the members of the group?

How will the banker gain the attention of individuals with different interests?

Clarifying the objective and gaining the interest of the members of the group are essential if sales calls with a group are to succeed. Feedback and evaluations from hundreds of individuals who participated in meetings indicated that they did not know the specific objective of a large number of the meetings they attended beforehand, and that their speakers did not clearly define the objectives to the group. A five-second statement of the objective is not sufficient, nor is merely stating the topic. Too often assumptions concerning the purpose of the meeting are made, and the assumptions lead to a breakdown in communications.

Too often bankers assume that the participants know exactly why they are there. If internal communications were not clear, bankers may have the full responsibility of explaining the background and preparing the group for the sales call. Bankers should take *several minutes* to define the objective and to sell the idea that the objective is of value to the group before beginning to discuss the topic or product. In group as well as one-on-one sales calls, bankers should find and hit Motivation Levers before they begin to sell. For example, a banker making a presentation to a board of directors concerning an International Balance Reporting System might state:

. . . This morning I would like to discuss a possible way to *reduce idle balances* and put those *balances* to *work* by investing them in multinational money market instruments. As you know, unless you can identify the *funds that are available* in time for you to use the information, you cannot *maximize short-term investment opportunities.* Before I discuss how our bank's Balance Reporting System may . . . I would like to *review* the present method. . . . As I understand it. . . .	Stating objective in terms that interest the customer.

Tying it to an assumed Motivation Lever.

Restating objective and hinting at benefits.

Benefits

Summary and building comparison (using research in a positive manner). |
| *or* Before I discuss how . . . could you tell me what you see as your . . . so that I can talk about the specifics of our . . . ? | Giving customers opportunity to articulate their needs. (Motivation Lever) |

Features and Benefits

Bankers should link features to benefits and should focus on the features and benefits that relate to the assumed Motivation Levers if they are to keep the interest of the group. Since participants may not have the opportunity to ask questions concerning benefits that will accrue to them, bankers should spell out the benefits.

Objection and Response

Since customers in a group may not have the time, opportunity, or inclination to raise objections, bankers should anticipate the objections that are likely to be raised in the minds of the participants. By building objections and responses into their presentations, bankers can reduce customer resistance. For example, "Some of you may be concerned about the other bank's willingness to provide us with the balance information. . . ."

Probing Questions

To maximize involvement, it is preferable that members of the group be free to ask questions throughout the sales call; however, when larger numbers are present, this can be difficult, and it is often necessary to suggest a question-and-answer period toward the conclusion of the sales presentation. Bankers should leave ample time for the question-and-answer period and *announce at the beginning* of their presentation how questions will be handled. In addition to using questions from the group to explain the product, bankers can include rhetorical or thought-provoking questions in their presentations in order to explain, clarify, and stimulate involvement. An example of such a question would be: "How many dollars are sitting idly because data cannot be gathered in time for you to make investment decisions?"

Constructive Listening

Although there is not that much opportunity to listen to the customers during the group presentation itself, the yellow-pad meetings should have provided bankers with information they can use in constructing a listening-based presentation. With the information gathered prior to the group meeting, bankers can incorporate interests, phrases, and ideas that are relevant to the group. Particular attention should be paid to questions that are asked during the presentation or during the question-and-answer period, since they provide bankers with the opportunity to satisfy customer concerns. After answering the question, *bankers should remember to check with the participant that in fact his or her question was satisfactorily answered.* For example, a question as simple as "Does that answer your concern [or question]?" can ensure that the question was adequately covered, and it signals to the group that the next issue can be raised.

Incremental Close and Incremental Summary

Bankers can use incremental summaries to supplement the incremental close and to develop understanding and agreement as they proceed through their presentation. Since participants may not be familiar with the context, there is a danger that they may become confused or distracted.

Incremental summaries serve to keep them alert and informed. Bankers should also use a final summary before initiating the action step.

Action Step

Just as in a one-on-one sales call, bankers should aim for getting the business. They should plan the desired action step prior to making the presentation. The action step is usually initiated by the banker but can be initiated by one of the participants, usually the decision maker. If there is a question-and-answer period at the end of the presentation, bankers should complete that period *before* initiating the action step. The reason for this is to establish as much clarity as possible among participants before seeking commitment to the product or service.

Body Signals

Reading and responding to body signals is much more difficult in group presentations, since they are multiplied by the number of participants. The banker's own body signals are also important, and so is maintaining eye contact with the group rather than focusing on the key decision makers(s) or reading notes. With a group it is important to be enthusiastic without being overly animated in hand or body gestures. (See pages 101–104 for a discussion of body signals.)

Sales Environment

The size of the group often influences the selection of the sales environment. Bankers should find out the kind of facility that will be used and the kind of seating arrangements that will be available. When given the choice, bankers should avoid the lock-horns position (sitting directly across from one another), particularly with the decision maker. They should also position themselves as a part of the group rather than apart from it, for example, by sitting with the board during the presentation (unless using or writing on a flip chart) rather than standing apart.

Summary

Sales presentations to a group can be demanding, but they can also be rewarding. Preparation through yellow-pad meetings and planning is important if sales results are to be achieved. The ten elements essential in a one-on-one sales call also apply in group sales situations, except that they require some modification to compensate for the increase in numbers. Exhibit 3 is an action planner that can be used by bankers in planning sales presentations to groups.

MANAGING THE DECISION-MAKING UNIT

"High and wide" is a sales strategy that refers to maximizing selling opportunities by earning the confidence and support of the *economic decision maker(s), decision influencers,* and the *user/influencer decision maker(s)* of a company. The economic decision maker is the high-level contact who has control of the purse strings, and the influencer or user decision maker is frequently a key person in management or in the technical or operational staff who has substantial influence on the economic decision maker's views because of his or her responsibilities and/or operational knowledge.

Decision Maker and Influencer

Bankers frequently meet with the vice-president of finance (high); unless the bankers also arrange to meet with individuals such as the comptroller or cash manager (wide) and satisfy their needs and concerns, the sale can be *undone internally* by staff members who may undermine the proposal because they were not involved in the decision and feel ignored, threatened, or confused. It is particularly important for line bankers to make these contacts and introduce their counterparts from a product area of the bank if opportunities to cross-sell and expand relationships are to be maximized.

Since senior people often rely heavily on operational staff for input, when marketing a product that will affect an internal system or require internal changes, bankers should involve and win over the technical staff. Since managers might not think of involving the key operational staff, it

Exhibit 3 Sales Planner for Presentation to a Group

Product: _____

Banker's Objective: _____

Customers' Assumed Motivation Levers: _____

Time: _____   Decision Maker(s): _____

Date: _____   Number of Customers: _____

                                  Customers' Roles: _____

                                  Environment: _____

Opening

Key Features and Benefits

       Features   *Benefits*

Anticipated Objections and Responses

       Objections   *Responses*

Incremental Summaries and Points at Which Summaries Will Occur

Questions and Answers (Q and A throughout presentation or in a Q-and-A period)

   Anticipated Questions   *Responses*

Final Summary

Action Step

Materials

Practice, Critique, and Modifications

(After completing worksheet, banker should construct a presentation *outline* that can be referred to, not read, during the sales presentation.)

may be prudent for bankers to inquire whether it would be appropriate to meet with key operations people. These wide meetings can be very helpful, since they enable bankers to gather information as well as marshall support.

For example, in discussing a new Account Reconcilement System bankers may ask, "What are your thoughts on my meeting with your cash manager to discuss. . . ?" or "When we meet with our specialists, are there any members of your staff that you would like to have at the meeting?" or "Shall I stop by and introduce myself and. . . ?" Very often the technical person can provide the data that are needed to establish a cost–benefit ratio, and will also be active in the installation of the product. By developing a relationship with the user decision makers as well as the economic decision makers, bankers can develop multilevel penetration in the company that will be helpful in advancing their ideas.

Influencer and Decision Maker

By the same token, if the banker's initial contact is from the operational (wide) end, every effort should be made to meet with senior (high) management. This meeting can be between management and the banker alone, or with the wide contact, the high contact and the banker. It is always preferable to arrange a direct meeting with the economic decision maker or the economic and the influencing decision maker, but sometimes for internal or political reasons, influencers may choose to act as the intermediary for the bankers. To protect the rapport and relationship established, bankers often must accept this. Whenever possible, they should diplomatically prepare materials that their contact can use or work with their contact in preparing for the presentation. In situations in which it is essential that bankers meet with senior-level personnel and they are unable to get past influencers, soliciting the support and involvement of a senior officer from the bank (executive vice-president or senior vice-president) for a joint call often automatically elevates the level of penetration without ruffling feathers.

Summary

Understanding how a customer makes decisions is the first step in managing the decision-making process. Bankers should utilize one contact in the company to meet other appropriate contacts. *Any time one member of the decision-making team makes references to checking with another, bankers should inquire about the possibility of arranging a meeting with the new contact so that they can tell their own story.* It is also very helpful gingerly to question the present contact about the attitudes and background of the new contact *prior to* meeting with him or her.

High and wide selling is an excellent strategy for building long-term relationships. Changes in management and promotions are also good reasons for utilizing a multicontact approach, to ensure that a relationship does not become seriously weakened of one change in personnel.

SALES MATERIALS

Professional and attractive sales brochures, exhibits, visuals, and sales aids can be used to increase the communication between bankers and their customers. They can be used during the sales call to imprint key points on the customer's mind, to illustrate complicated points, or to provide customers with examples of the content and format of reports. They also can be used as leave behind pieces that can reinforce a particular idea after the sales call has been completed.

Sales Brochures

Brochures are a reflection on the bank; therefore they should be professional and attractive. Divisions of the bank should coordinate their customer-directed materials so that they convey a unified bankwide image rather than a series of unrelated images.

Just as bankers should evaluate the appearance of sales brochures in determining whether or not to use them, they should evaluate the content. The content of the brochures should reflect a consultative sales approach. Too often sales materials focus exclusively on the operations and features of the product from the bank's point of view without addressing benefits or value to the customer for whom they have been written. By addressing the bank's needs, features, and accomplishments, they fail to provide customers with information relevant to their needs. Unless brochures include in-house capabilities of the products (features) along with the value of the product to the customer (benefits), *they will not generate customer interest*. Unfortunately, because many brochures focus on features or benefits to the bank instead of benefits to the customer, they are relegated to the wastebasket. If customers are expected to utilize and refer to leave-behind pieces after the sales call or respond positively to them during the sales call, they should be pertinent to customers' needs and situations. Bankers should use brochures that reflect customers' points of view to clarify and reinforce their products, and should not waste their time with materials that lack such customer orientation.

Sales Aids

Sales aids (flip charts, slides, charts, brochures, etc.) are materials that can be used during a sales call to assist bankers in communicating with their customers. Generally bankers are reluctant to use sales aids, since they seem reminiscent of door-to-door or canned selling. This attitude is unfortunate, because they can be used in an individualized and consultative way and can be of particular value in selling environment in which there is a wide range of products. They are most effective when they incorporate customer feedback through probing questions. For example, in showing a plan for the acceleration of cash flow through a Lock Box, bankers should ask, "How would this improved availability of funds assist your company in meeting its daily cash needs?" Bankers should use the customer's comments to pinpoint and relate benefits in terms of dollars, time, and convenience. Sales aids can be used for basic products and also for sophisticated products. A multinational netting system, for example, can be explained much more simply with a diagram than with words alone.

Sales aids, exhibits, and visuals can help customers understand and appreciate the features and benefits of a product. By showing examples of reports and the kind of information provided, customers can get hands-on-experience with the product.

Other Sales Aids

In addition to brochures and sales aids, there are several special materials that can be of significant value to bankers when they are used properly. They are the specification summary and the bank's annual or quarterly report.

Specification Summaries

Specification summaries, information checklists that outline the information needed to implement a product, are excellent selling and cross-selling aids. A specification summary should be developed for each product that *requires analysis by a specialist or technical support from the* operations area. During the sales interview or immediately before or after the action step, bankers can use specification summaries to gather data to be provided to the specialists, or to operations. The information from the specification summary should be used to outline the customer's requirements and to communicate the implementation instructions to operations.

Specification summaries can also be given to specialists to help them prepare for a joint call with the banker. When used for referral purposes they should be forwarded by bankers to the specialists.

Specification summaries should include the following information:

1 Corporate information
   Name: _____
   Address: _____   Phone: _____
   Decision maker: _____
   Operational contact: _____
   Type of business: _____
2 Product information
   Product: _____
   Relevant Data for Each Product (i.e., for Direct Deposit: number of employees, frequency of deposit, data input, delivery location; for Foreign Exchange: currencies, amount of foreign exchange activity ($), and suggested Foreign Exchange line; for Import Letter of Credit; number L/Cs monthly, mix of time and sight, and countries)
   Options: _____
   Customer Requirements: _____
3 Operations Interface between Bank and Customer
   Banker (account officer): _____
   Bank Specialists: _____
   Customer Contact: _____
   Implementation Date: _____
   Special Instructions: _____

Each product should have its own specification summary, outlining the specific data required for each product. A standardized specification summary cannot be used for all products, since the product information category for each product will vary. Used correctly, the specification summary can be an effective and formal referral document to the specialist or operations area assigned to the product.

The Annual or Quarterly Report

The bank's annual report can be an excellent leave-behind piece. It is particularly useful when bankers are calling in locations that may not be familiar with the bank or when they are discussing products such as Commercial Paper or other investment instruments. Bankers should distribute annual reports when they are ready to utilize them or at the conclusion of the meeting, so that customers are not distracted by them.

Distribution of All Handouts/Sales Aids

Bankers should selectively choose handouts that they will use and should consciously control the distribution. Unless bankers decide beforehand when and how materials will be distributed and used, they may find themselves in competition with their own handouts for the customer's attention. When distributing handouts, bankers should:

1 Distribute handouts *as they are to be used, not before,* since the customer may focus on the sales material rather than on what the banker is saying.
2 Introduce and explain what the handout is and why it is being distributed.
3 For a larger group, state method and time of distribution.
4 Avoid wasting too much time distributing materials.

Summary

To get maximum effect with all sales materials, bankers should:

1 Be thoroughly familiar with any materials to be used to ensure that they are pertinent and accurate.

2   Place materials *in the order* in which they will be used.

3   Customize materials whenever possible (company's name, date of meeting, clipping on of business card in advance).

4   Maintain control over printed material by distributing it *as it will be used,* not before, since it will distract the customer's attention from the sales interview.

5   Leave appropriate materials behind or send them as a follow-up.

Sales materials can be excellent reinforcement tools. They can highlight or document particular points and can assist bankers in explaining their ideas. They should be used to support bankers in their sales effort but never to replace them or to substitute for a sales interview.

Sales materials can complement the consultative banking approach when they are written from the customer's point of view. Effective sales materials can increase the customer's understanding of a product and serve as a reminder of potential value, improvement, or opportunity to him or her when they are used by bankers in an individualized and timely fashion.

4

*Developing
and Managing
Relationships*

Today everyone is talking about *relationship banking*. This reflects a highly competitive environment that is composed of sophisticated customers whose needs cover a broad range of products and services. Because of the changing regulatory environment and also advanced technology, banks are now able to provide these products and services. In delivering their total resources, bankers must consider not only the present needs of the customer but also his or her long-range needs so that they can build mutually profitable long-term relationships.

Today's banker is no longer exclusively a lender but is also a manager who must monitor not only the customer's credit needs but also his or her noncredit needs. A banker must make sure that the bank's total calling effort is addressing all of the customer's needs—investments, trust, cash management, trade. To do this, it has become essential that bankers know and monitor not only their traditional contacts in a company, but also *all* key decision makers and influencers. Unless they do this, competitors will make inroads to their customers. Of course, as they manage the lending and nonlending customer relationship, bankers have the added responsibility of making certain that the bank is being properly compensated for the full spectrum of services it is providing.

Developing relationship strategies, sales planning, sales, and follow-up are key factors in relationship building. Although this book does not address developing long-range relationship strategies, it addresses the first essential step in the sales planning process: prospecting.

PROSPECTING

The term *prospecting* was first used during the gold rush of 1849 to describe the search for promising places to find gold. Prospecting for bankers is faithful to its original definition, "looking for a place that may be profitably worked." A prospect may be an *existing* customer who is eligible for complementary or additional products, services, or credit, or a *new* individual or company with the potential of becoming a customer. Prospecting involves actively searching out and developing new business sources. Prospecting is the action step that follows sales planning; it is the implementation of a sales plan.

134

Sales planning means setting goals and objectives, developing strategies, and establishing an evaluation system to be used in measuring results and defining new goals. *Sales* involves prospecting, selling, implementing, and following up. The bridge between sales planning and selling is the prospect list. Developing the prospect list is planning, and acting on the prospect list is selling.

Developing a Prospect List

One of the key sales planning strategies is the development and organization of a viable prospect list. Bankers should identify their market area and determine the types of companies that make up their target market. Once they identify their market, bankers should develop their prospect lists.

Some resources that bankers can use in constructing their prospect lists are:

Bank's own market research and planning unit (files, records, research)

Bank's senior management or other bankers (contacts with the bank)

Present customers (These are the best source of new business.)

Dormant accounts ("I know you had a relationship with us, and I'd like to take a fresh look and find out. . . .")

Customers or suppliers of present customers

Competitors of customers

Companies with a new management team or new financial manager

Published materials (such as reports, trade magazines, journals, business pages in newspapers, annual reports, *Ayers Directory,* Fortune 500 and 1000, Dun and Bradstreet, Moody's, Standard & Poor's, *Who's Who*)

News clippings

Chambers of commerce

Other professionals (lawyers, accountants who are windows to other customers)

Referrals from customers (Ask present customers with pad and pen in hand.)

Colleagues, organizations, professional groups, clubs, personal friends

Directories in buildings (cold canvass or cold calling)

Telephone directories (commercial)

Smokestacking (driving or walking around and observing business development)

Prospect lists should be updated with deletions and additions periodically. A prospect profile card should be developed for each entry. Some basic information to include is:

1 Name of company or business
2 Officers' names and functions
3 Relationship with the bank
4 Annual sales volume
5 Total number of employees and number of employees on site
6 Zip code (Plan calls by zip code to cluster calls.)
7 Needs
8 Contact dates

Developing a prospect list is a part of planning, not selling. The phrase *prospect list* may be misleading, because the names appearing on the list are really *"suspects"*; they become prospects after they are rated and approached.

Rating Prospects

Bankers should rate their prospects if they want to maximize the hours they spend on prospect calls. The following criteria can be used to assist bankers in rating their prospects and developing their priorities.

1 Prospect's eligibility for credit or noncredit business
2 Identity of decision maker(s)
3 Prospect's known needs
4 Banker's industry expertise
5 Banker's knowledge of products utilized in the industry
6 Banker's introduction (third-party?)

7 Bank's reputation in the industry

8 Bank's competitive standing

9 Bank's lead over the competition

10 Prospect's borrowing potential or need for noncredit

11 Prospect's potential profitability

12 Time estimate for getting business (days, months, years)

13 Needs not satisfied by company's present bank(s)

14 Total value of the relationship

Prospect Ratio

Bankers have to determine the number of prospects they should meet with to achieve their objectives so that they can schedule their sales activities. Certainly the names on the prospect list should far exceed the number of calls to be made. But bankers should determine their own prospect ratio (hit ratio of number of prospects to be contacted to make a sale). Regardless of the factors that influence it (market, competition, etc.), bankers should strive to track the number of calls made to the number of sales made, so they know their true batting average.

Factors that bankers can consider in developing their prospect ratios are:

Dollar Objective for New Business—Dollar amount to be achieved over the next year.

New Customers or Expanded Business with Present Customers Needed to Achieve Objective for New Business. (Determine average value of a customer by dividing total dollar value of all customers by the total number of present customers and then divide that figure into the goal for new business.

Number of New Prospects to Approach to Gain an Interview. Determine the number of prospects that must be approached or called to get an appointment for a sales interview.

Number of Sales Presentations to Produce One New Customer. Determine from experience approximately how many prospects must be seen to produce one new customer.

Using a modification of this approach, bankers should be able to approximate how many sales calls should be made to achieve their objectives.

Bankers should determine through experience and assessment of results what their sales ratios are and how they compare to those of other bankers. This is one of the most valuable kinds of information bankers can have, since it enables them to compare and evaluate results and make modifications in scheduling or planning; it also helps bankers set new objectives. This kind of organized prospecting effort results in a sales effort that is more efficient and effective.

Ways to Prospect

Prospecting is the first step in developing new relationships or expanding present ones; or it involves actively searching out and developing business opportunities. A prospect may be an *existing customer* who is eligible for complementary or additional noncredit or credit products or services. Existing customers are the best and often most profitable source of new business. Depending on market and relationship penetration and the bank's marketing plan, bankers should determine what percentage of their sales time should be spent increasing business with present customers. A prospect may also be a *new individual or company* with the potential of becoming a customer. Of course, it is more difficult to prospect with *new* individuals or companies; therefore prospecting for new relationships will be the primary focus of this chapter. Using their prospect lists or a cold-canvass approach, bankers basically have two alternative ways to prospect: the appointment call, or the cold call (a call without an appointment). Regardless of which method they use, follow-up is critical.

Appointment Calls

It is recommended that bankers arrange appointments in advance. This is particularly appropriate with corporate customers; with small neighborhood businesses or with personal banking customers, it may be more acceptable to make cold calls.

The telephone is the most efficient tool for arranging appointments. When calling for an appointment, bankers should, in most circumstances, avoid the temptation to sell over the telephone with noncustomers. Except for Foreign Exchange, Money Desk Transactions, and so on, the telephone should be used to arrange an appointment and no more! The opportunity to meet a customer in person should not be lost by trying the almost impossible (to qualify, interest, explain, probe, sell, and complete the sale) over the telephone. In making the telephone contact with a prospect, the banker's objective should be only to *arrange an appointment*.

Making the Telephone Appointment

To maximize the benefits of the telephone, bankers should appreciate its strengths as well as its limitations. As one of its major strengths, the telephone is an invaluable time saver for arranging to meet with prospects. Bankers should also recognize the limitations of the telephone and limit their conversations to the kind of information included in the opening of their sales calls, in which they *sell the appointment, and not the product*. At all costs—and it will probably cost the appointment—bankers should avoid the trap of trying to sell over the telephone.

Appointment telephone calls with prospects should be limited to:

1 Greeting.
2 Identifying banker and bank.
3 Using hinge (mutual point of reference).
4 Stating possible *value* to customer in seeing banker (based on research or experience or even an educated guess).
5 Requesting the initial appointment.
6 Establishing date, time, and place.
7 Confirming date to tie down the appointment.
8 Repeating name (''For your calendar, my name is. . . . '' [Spell it].

Sometimes, if bankers do not have qualifying information on the customer, they may find it necessary to ask some qualifying questions after stating the possible value.

Telephone Brush-off Objections

Because of prospects' busy schedules and competitive and business pressures, prospects may *resist* scheduling the appointment and offer "brush-off" objections. Typical objections are:

"I'm too busy."
"Send me a proposal."
"My bank provides everything."
"Tell me over the phone what you want, to save time."
"Call _____ , who reports to me."
"We just changed banks."

When prospects pose smoke-screen objections or excuses, they are often really saying, "You haven't convinced me there is an advantage for *me* in seeing you." The customer does not really want a dissertation on the product, but does want to know how he or she will benefit from the meeting. In attempting to resolve the objection, bankers should guard against selling over the phone and avoid a lengthy product or idea discussion. Since bankers themselves are the most important factor in communicating information, they should not rely on the telephone voices alone to establish rapport, credibility, or substitute for the time necessary for an effective sales interview.

The 15-Minute Strategy. When bankers are faced with brush-off objections, they should use the "15-minute strategy" in which they repeat the objection, restate the possible advantages that may accrue to the prospect through the sales meeting, and suggest a 15-minute or half-hour introductory appointment.

   This strategy should be used after a prospect rejects the idea of the appointment. Bankers should:

1   Repeat the objection.
2   Restate the possible value to the customer (based on homework).
3   Repeat request for the appointment but add a 15-minute time frame.
4   Establish a date and time.

5 Confirm date and time.

6 Repeat name.

The obvious difference between the first request for an appointment and the second request following the customer's objection is the introduction of the limited 15-minute time frame. Very often customers will agree to an initial meeting that has tight parameters. Bankers should not lose sight of their main objective, which is to arrange a personal appointment.

The following are examples of using the telephone to sell the interview and not the product after the customer gives a brush-off objection:

Objections	Consultative Telephone Response
I'm not interested.	Mr. _____ , I can understand your not being interested in . . . , since you have not had a chance to discuss how it may be possible to . . . . I would like to meet with you to discuss with you how it may . . . for your company. I think if we could meet for 15 minutes, you could determine . . . . Would later this week be convenient or early next week? Tuesday morning at 9:30 or Wednesday at 11:00?
I'm too busy.	Mrs. _____ , I can appreciate that you have a busy schedule and that is why I called. I'd like to arrange a 15-minute appointment at your convenience to discuss the way in which . . . could possibly . . . so that you could determine whether a full appointment . . . . Would . . . ?
Tell me what your idea is.	Miss _____ , . . . can be explained clearly and quickly, but by meeting with you for 15 minutes, I could relate it more specifically to your requirements. What time would be convenient for a brief meeting?
Your bank wasn't interested in my business four years ago. You got frightened of my industry and wouldn't talk to me.	I'm sorry to hear that you had that experience with our bank. I'd appreciate the opportunity to meet with you for 15 minutes and discuss the possible ways in which . . . now. I think you will find the bank has changed and . . . . Would next week be a convenient time for a meeting?
Send me a proposal.	I will be very happy to send you the information, Mr. _____ , but I would like to meet with you for 15 minutes to ensure that the materials are

appropriate for your particular situation. Would
. . . ? (One very successful banker says, "I don't
know enough about your business to send a proposal. I think it could be to our mutual advantage
if we could sit down and talk about. . . . ")

I can't afford it right now.

Mrs. _____ , I can understand your desire to
avoid unnecessary expenses; however, it may be
to your advantage to review . . . to determine
whether or not it can offset . . . and possibly
reduce . . . . Would . . . ?

You'll be wasting your
time.

I appreciate your consideration; however, it is my
feeling that it will take only 15 minutes to determine the value of . . . to you. Would . . . ?

I've just changed banks.

I can understand your commitment to a new relationship, but I would appreciate the opportunity
to meet with you for 15 minutes so that you can
determine the extent to which we may be able to
complement your present banking relationship.
. . .

My present bank provides
everything.

I can appreciate that you have a banking relationship that is satisfying your current needs. I'd like
to meet with you for 15 minutes, to discuss . . .
so that you can determine [compare] the possible
advantages to you and the way we could possibly
complement your present relationship. When
could we get together later this week?

You'll have to call _____ ,
my assistant.

I would appreciate the opportunity to meet with
_____ . I will contact her and keep you abreast
of the progress. I hope to have the opportunity to
meet with you to present . . . after the initial
meeting. [A letter should be sent thanking the
customer for arranging or suggesting the meeting
and also outlining benefits that *may* accrue to the
customer as a result of the meeting. Also if possible bankers should introduce themselves during
the call and should send a follow-up letter.]
If the customer is really the one the banker
should see due to distance or corporate input:
Mr. _____ , I would welcome the opportunity
to meet with _____ . Since I will be there, I
would also like to stop in and introduce myself
to you after seeing _____ to . . . . [This is high
and wide selling in which bankers can use the
information gathered during the wide meeting to
sell to high personnel.]

These examples are provided to encourage bankers to make a second effort, not of course to be read or used verbatim.

Getting the appointment with a prospect is often determined by the banker's ability to suggest a *possible* opportunity to the prospect. Each of the blanks in the responses indicated that the bankers did some homework prior to the call. Bankers should work toward setting a brief initial appointment and should use their appointment time to motivate the prospect to extend the time or to set a full appointment. Once bankers succeed in setting the appointment, they should use their 15 minutes to find out about the prospect's situation, uncover the prospect's needs, and interest the prospect sufficiently in what the bank may be able to do for him or her so that a *full* appointment is set or the present one is extended. When the 15 minutes are up, bankers should acknowledge this and ask if they should continue, or if a second appointment would be more convenient.

The objections and responses show how bankers can keep sight of their objective to sell a personal sales interview and to retain control of the telephone conversation. Trying to sell on the telephone often results in lost opportunities. "Proposals in the mail" and other nondirect approaches are time-consuming and expensive, and their results are often disappointing. Personal first interviews usually cannot be replaced by phone calls, proposals, or letters.

Telephone Techniques

To help secure appointments with prospects, bankers can also incorporate the following telephone techniques.

Confidence. By writing out the key points of the opening and practicing to ensure that they comunicate with confidence, bankers can influence a positive response from customers.

Assumptive Opening with Secretaries. When speaking to secretaries, bankers should assume that they will get through to the party they are calling. Rather than asking to speak to Mr. Smith, bankers should say, "Mr. Smith, please. Tom Brown calling." If Mr. Smith is not available, bankers should jot down the secretary's name and use it during the next call.

Third-Party Referral Openings. Referrals from a satisfied customer, acquaintances, or another third party are invaluable to bankers who are prospecting. "Mr. X suggested I contact you. . . . "

Hinge Openings.   Referring to an article in the paper about a new facility, new management, or any point of reference that serves to connect bankers with customers is also an effective way to open. "In your annual report. . . ."

Industry Opening.   Stating experience with the customer's industry also can motivate a customer to set an appointment. "I have been working with several manufacturing companies. . . ."

New Development Opening.   Discussing a new situation or a new product or any change or innovation in the bank or in the company is an excellent way to open. "Our bank has just become a member of X banking group, increasing our ability to provide international services."

General Strategies.   Some general strategies for arranging an appointment are:

Send a letter to a difficult-to-reach prospect before the telephone call and use the letter as a hinge in selling the appointment. (Particularly helpful for priority are prospects to have the letter come from a senior bank offering to a senior in the company and to make the first call a joint call.)

Develop rapport with secretaries; ask for and use their names. (Write names on Rolodex and in the prospect information file.)

Don't try to sell the product—sell the interview.

Use third-party references whenever possible.

Refer to a similar client using your service.

Suggest a new or special aspect of a product.

Suggest a 15-minute time frame or shorter for a new prospect after a brush-off objection.

Repeat objections before fielding them to show concern for the customer.

Avoid falling into a brush-off trap of sending a proposal without an interview to determine needs.

Meet with someone from the decision maker's staff if necessary as a first step.

The Cold Call

The second most frequently used method of prospecting is the cold call. A cold call is a personal visit to a prospect *without an appointment.* Experience with bankers indicates that there is confusion concerning the definition of a cold call. Some bankers think it is a call for which they are unprepared, or a first call. Basically, bankers should not waste their time on calls for which they are unprepared. Cold calls as they are used in this book refer to meeting with prospective or established customers that were not arranged in advance.

Cold calls have a limited place in certain banking situations. The can never replace appointment calls, but they can *supplement* them. The appointment call is considered more professional with corporate customers and it is certainly more effective and time efficient.

Why then bother with the cold call? For several key reasons:

1   In some markets it is appropriate (some correspondent banks, personal trust bankers, lower middle market).
2   Bankers can maximize prime-time selling by substituting the cold call for canceled or interrupted appointment calls.
3   The cold call increases banker's ability to maximize a market area in an out-of-the-way location and ensure the most complete coverage of an area.
4   The cold call is perceived positively in some markets as aggressive.
5   The cold call is an excellent way to fill the time gap between appointment calls, become better acquainted with market areas, and learn about customers and competition.
6   The cold call provides an opportunity to gather specific information about the company from talking to receptionists, reading annual reports, personally seeing the facility, and so on.
7   The cold call provides inexperienced bankers with hands-on experience with customers and the marketplace.
8   The cold call is a kind of welcome wagon for new small businesses in the area.
9   The cold call can be used to arrange full appointments.

Limited Objective of the Cold Call.   Although cold calls can be used successfully to round out the banker's schedule and to create a market presence, they are fraught with frustrations and disappointments. The most negative aspects of cold calls are the high rate of rejection and refusal and the misuse of time. Cold calls on existing customers are often more accepted or tolerated than cold calling on prospects. Prospects often respond negatively to cold calls because they consider them to be second-rate calls that do not show respect or concern for the prospect or his or her schedule. Nevertheless, cold calls can be valuable *when they are approached with realistic objectives.* When bankers initiate cold calls anticipating immediate results, they are building in their own disappointment, failure, and disillusionment. Although there are some war stories of major accounts being obtained as a result of a cold call, most cold calls are not so instantly productive. *Cold calls should be used not to sell a product but rather to uncover needs and sell the idea of the next full appointment. The primary objective for cold calls should be to arrange a full appointment to address the customer's needs.*

Cold calls generally should be used: to identify key contacts; to gather names; to identify possible needs; to collect brochures, in-house literature, annual reports, and other such material; and to set a full appointment. If a banker meets with a prospect and something develops because of the banker's inventiveness, the timeliness of the call, the prospect's immediate need, or his or her dissatisfaction with a current banking relationship, the banker should take advantage of the opportunity, recognizing that the results exceeded the initial objective. Unless the limited objective of the cold call is understood, cold calling can do more damage to morale than can be offset by the amount of business developed. Like the telephone prospect call, the cold call should aim at *setting a full appointment.*

Cold Call Objections.   Just as prospects object over the telephone, prospects or their secretaries often resist meeting with bankers during a cold call. As with the telephone call, bankers should not attempt a full sales call when resistance is shown, but rather should use the brief meeting with the secretary or the prospect briefly to find facts, gather some names, identify needs, hint at some possible benefits, and *set a full appointment* for another date. If an appointment cannot be set at the time, bankers should leave their cards, send a follow-up letter, telephone the prospect, and use the cold call as the hinge for setting a full appointment.

Persistence and patience are important in making cold calls. Whether it is a receptionist, secretary, assistant, or the prospect himself or herself who puts up a smoke-screen objection to avoid the sales interview, it is the banker's task to earn the customer's attention and time. Making the cold call, leaving business cards, sending follow-up letters, or making follow-up calls all increase the likelihood of getting a full appointment. Cold calls are demanding, but when they are used to *supplement* appointment calls, they can be a challenging and rewarding way to gain experience and increase market share.

Summary

Appointment calls supplemented with cold calls provide an effective approach to prospecting. Follow-through is the heart of all prospecting activities, and a simple, workable follow-up system that triggers follow-up calls is critical. In sales, time is money, and the time spent in prospecting, identifying prospects, qualifying them, and meeting with them is an investment that can result in new and expanded relationships.

THE TELEPHONE AS A RELATIONSHIP MANAGEMENT TOOL

Telephones are indispensable sales planning and follow-up tools. They are time savers that should be used to:

Set appointments.

Maintain contact with current customers.

Keep contact with inactive customers.

Reactivate accounts.

Respond to inquiries.

Address and solve customer problems.

Check on progress or decisions.

Gather information.

Qualify customers and prospects.

Follow up on accounts.

Prospect.

Improve internal communications with operations or specialists.

Solve internal and external emergency or long-distance problems.

Check names, titles, addresses, and so on. Cross-sell to present customers.

Telephone contact should not be used to substitute for personal, face-to-face contact. However, because of time pressure, distance, and travel expense, many bankers find that they are required to sell, particularly when negotiating and closing deals, over the telephone. When this is necessary, bankers should:

Initiate the telephone contact or call the customer back if he or she is not prepared.

Have needed material, files, and so on available during the call.

Take notes. (Customers do).

Practice using a squawk box. (Ask who is there.)

When bankers hold conference telephone calls with customers, they should make sure that they are close enough to each other to keep eye contact and pass notes.

Some products, such as Money Desk products, lend themselves to telephone selling, but most bank products require initial face-to-face contact and follow-up. The primary role of the telephone is as a tool for management and development of the relationship.

Planning, and homework should precede all telephone calls. Preparation is important if the time, effort, and potential of telephoning are to be realized. Bankers should be prepared with names, titles, dates, and *data*. They should call from a relatively quiet and uninterrupted place and should take notes about the specifics of the conversation. Unless there are absolutely no alternatives, phone booths should be avoided in setting appointments or calling customers, since note-taking space and necessary information are often unavailable. Also bankers should flip through their Rolodexes and tickler files each month to make sure they are maximizing present opportunities and following up as promised or required. The telephone can be a powerful sales planning and follow-up tool. It can set the stage, monitor progress, and nurture the relationship.

Telephones are time savers when used to prospect, set appointments, and follow up on sales calls. Experience shows that *for direct sales for bankers,* and for serious problem solving, face-to-face selling is preferable. Nothing can replace the personal visit; however, the telephone can be used to begin and maintain a sales dialogue and reach agreements when face-to-face is not possible because of distance and time factors. When using the telephone to sell it is important to make a checklist prior to the call, take notes during the call, and confirm agreements in writing. *Used properly, the telephone wire can be a lifeline of the sale—starting it, holding it together, and holding on to it.*

NURTURING THE ACCOUNT

The relationship begins *after* an agreement has been reached and the contract has been signed. Relationships must be cultivated and nurtured if they are to survive. The objective of nurturing is to maintain and expand relationships and to establish long-term relationships that are beneficial to the customer and the bank. Nurturing is an important part of relationship management, since it is the vehicle for follow-up, cross-selling, problem solving, and overall account maintenance. One of the most important functions of bankers in cultivating the relationship is to monitor the decision makers and the organizational structure. They should also monitor the total calling effort of the bank to maximize the full profit potential of the relationship.

Follow-up

Follow-up is a mechanism for ensuring customer satisfaction and therefore is essential to relationship management. As relationship managers, bankers should function as a liaison between the customer and the bank to facilitate a smooth start for a new product or service and to monitor the activities of their relationships. If problems arise, bankers should solve them to provide customers with the service and personal attention they require. *Consistent, effective follow-up is the weakest link in all businesses.* Bankers who provide their customers with efficient and timely follow-up and follow-through are almost always guaranteed of creating their own competitive edge over a large segment of their competitors. To facilitate follow-up, bankers should update their records and complete call reports immediately (within 24 hours) after the call, initiate appropriate internal contacts with product areas, develop internal leverage for credit approval, respond in a timely manner, and record monitoring and follow-up activities in their own calendars to trigger future activities. Follow-up actions can include providing information to the customer, setting an appointment with a specialist, or installing a product. If there is no specific follow-up, bankers should put a notation in a tickler file and initiate the next personal or telephone nurturing call within a reasonable time span, usually at least once a quarter. Energies, progress, and opportunities can be wasted unless there is disciplined follow-up. Follow-up (a personal visit, telephone contact, a letter, clipping and sending of an article) is as important to sales as sales planning, the making of sales calls, or completing sales, particularly in a highly competitive environment. Follow-up separates professionals from everyone else.

Cross-Selling

Cross-selling is a valuable by-product of nurturing, since nurturing calls are an excellent way to recognize and maximize cross-selling opportunities. The term *cross-selling* refers to providing additional bank products and services to current customers.

All customers who have an account with the bank are targets for cross-selling. Nurturing provides a way to expand relationships, since present customers are the best sources of additional business. Customers who have a relationship with the bank may frequently benefit from products that complement their present systems or from new products that can meet their other financial and banking needs. For example, a customer who uses several of the bank's cash management products might be a good candidate for computerized balance reporting service, or for other corporate products such as Import Letter of Credit and Foreign Exchange. He or she also may be an excellent candidate for investment instruments such as Certificates of Deposit or Commercial Paper.

Cross-selling is a key factor in developing and keeping market share. Research has demonstrated that the *bond* between customers and the bank is strengthened significantly with each additional credit and noncredit product. Because of the changes in the banking industry, customers have begun to expect their banks to be able to satisfy the full spectrum of their financial needs. Bankers can capitalize on this by initiating ways to integrate services and increase customer convenience.

Cross-selling results are not a matter of luck or simply being at the right place at the right time. Bankers must create their own luck by broadening their range of product knowledge and refining their communication skills so that they can recognize and maximize the opportunities that exist with each of their customers. They should apply their product knowledge, customer knowledge, and consultative selling techniques to build relationships. To help bankers in their cross-selling efforts, banks often provide computerized systems that provide access to information on present customers, from which cross-selling opportunities can be determined. Pertinent information can be used to identify the customer's present relationship with the bank and to project cross-selling opportunities. If bankers do not have computerized resources, they should utilize whatever records are available.

To maximize cross-selling opportunities, bankers should understand how products complement one another and which products are utilized in particular industries. For example:

Customer	Industry	Current Products	Possible Cross-Selling Opportunities
X Company	Importer and exporter of soft goods	Letter of Credit (Import, Export)	Foreign Currency Trading (Foreign Exchange) Bankers Acceptance Foreign Exchange Advisory International Cash Management

Cross-selling solidifies long-term relationships. It is the vehicle for not only expanding market share but also keeping it. It helps bankers lock in their customers and block their competitors. In today's banking environment, banks are aggressively seeking one another's market share. The ongoing relationship that once existed in banking is not a part of the banking climate of today. Today's bankers must earn their customers' *loyalty by building a total banking relationship,* and they must help build in loyalty by satisfying needs through the cross-selling of credit and non-credit services. The obvious advantage of cross-selling, as a relationship strategy, particularly for priority accounts, is that it reduces the customer's need or desire to look to other financial institutions for financial services.

Nurturing Calls

Nurturing calls are calls on present customers. They are vital, since present customers are the best prospects.

Nurturing calls must be more than "what's new" or "hello calls". Too often bankers go unprepared for a nurturing call. The objective of the nurturing should be to identify and satisfy needs. Nurturing calls that do not result in uncovering problems may not uncover opportunities. *Bankers should look for problems*, bank related or company related. Bankers who can help solve problems that the customer has can strengthen and expand the business relationship. As problems are understood and addressed, bankers can make recommendations that satisfy customer needs, while at the same time they promote the products or services of the bank and profitably increase market share.

Nurturing calls require specific preparation. Bankers should refer to sales call reports, files, and records from their last call to analyze and evaluate the status of the relationship.

Bankers must complete call reports, not just to "push paper" but to keep track of the information that was gathered during the last contact. Memory should never be counted on at a later time. Far too much valuable information is lost when entrusted to memory. Call reports when they are completed and filed properly, can give bankers or their colleagues instant and complete recall.

As they open their nurturing call, bankers should:

Greet customer and establish rapport.

Summarize status to date.

Inquire about customer satisfaction.

State general objective.

Be prepared to look at the overview.

Seek customer comments on conditions or status by asking questions pertaining to the account or industry.

Look for problems.

If a problem arises: discuss problems, ask questions, provide data.

Meet with support personnel if necessary.

Plan next step or corrective step.

Be alert for opportunities to cross-sell.

Actively explore cross-selling opportunities.

Make and strengthen contacts in the company.

Utilize the ten elements of a sales call.

Establish and reaffirm the next step or date of next contact.

Summary

Nurturing is a part of sales planning, sales implementation, and sales maintenance. It is the sign of a healthy customer relationship. When nurturing, bankers reinforce the confidence that customers exhibited in choosing them and their bank in the first place. Nurturing strengthens established relationships and converts new accounts into a long-term relationship. Nurturing of accounts is a crucial step in expanding relationships. Bankers who nurture their accounts are less likely to lose them, and that of course is the objective of relationship banking.

5
Sales Tips

The sales tips that are listed in Exhibit 4 concern some of the areas in which both new and seasoned bankers often encounter difficulties during sales calls. These sales tips are based on observation, feedback, and critique of more than 1000 bankers in role-play situations as well as in actual sales situations.

Exhibit 4   Sales Tips

Area of Possible Difficulty	The Wrong Approach	Analysis	Improvement
Introduction on first prospect calls.	**Banker.** I'm Carmen Smith.	On first calls it is appropriate for bankers to give some information about their positions, division at the bank, and some information on the bank (three or four minutes is usually sufficient unless the customer expresses a desire for more information) and also to present cards (place cards conveniently for easy access).	**Banker.** I'm Carmen Smith, National Division, X Bank [presentation of card]. We . . . .
Presenting potential customer benefits.	**Banker.** We definitely have . . . . [**or**] We have a fantastic	It is better to position initial benefits with *may* or *possibly* when first introducing an idea to a customer. Exaggerated claims can damage credibility.	**Banker.** . . . to discuss the ways in which we *possibly* can . . . . [**or**] Our new service *may provide*. . . .

156

Exhibit 4   Sales Tips (continued)

Area of Possible Difficulty	The Wrong Approach	Analysis	Improvement
Understanding the customer's present situation and before selling.	**Banker.** We can improve your cash flow by	Before discussing a product, bankers should use probing questions to learn about their customers' or prospects' present system or situation and uncover needs. They should test the assumptions they made prior to meeting with the customer, and identify and verify needs before intiating a discussion of a product or offering solutions to problems.	**Banker.** Can you tell me how you are now collecting your remittances? . . . By utilizing our Lock Box. . . .
Asking questions.	**Banker.** How are you paying for your imports; from what countries do you import; and how satisfied are you with your suppliers?	It is better to ask *one* question at a time, rather than hook a series of questions together. A string of questions is confusing, and questions are apt to get lost. Questions can be specific or general, but they should be asked one at a time.	**Banker.** How are you paying for your imports? [**or**] Can you tell me a little about your importing operation?

Exhibit 4   Sales Tips (continued)

Area of Possible Difficulty	The Wrong Approach	Analysis	Improvement
Giving the customer the opportunity to answer questions.	**Banker.** What problems are you having? Are there delays, errors? What we have found is	Bankers should avoid answering their own questions, suggesting possible answers, or going into a long explanatory statement. By waiting patiently, bankers can give the customer an opportunity to respond. Although four or five seconds may seem like an eternity, they should learn to wait and be silent if they are to understand the customer's situation or point of view.	**Banker.** What problems are you having?
Responding to customer.	**Customer.** We certainly don't want to speculate. **Banker.** You can't call this speculating.	Rather than contradict the customer, it is preferable to be positive and build on what the customer says.	**Customer.** We certainly don't want to speculate. **Banker.** From what you have said, I can understand that speculation is the last thing. . . . We can help you eliminate the risk. . . .

Exhibit 4   Sales Tips (continued)

Area of Possible Difficulty	The Wrong Approach	Analysis	Improvement
Using competitive information.	**Banker.** Y Bank is known for its impersonal and poor service.	Direct attacks on other banks are unprofessional. It is better to bring out their weaknesses by questions or by making objection comparisons about specific features and benefits.	**Banker.** What has been your experience with Y Bank? How promptly do they [**or** can they] respond to your inquiries? We provide . . . .
Gathering competitive information.	**Customer.** We use two New York banks. **Banker.** We think we can provide	Bankers should find out who the competitors are, *what is included in the offer, and the price*, to compare price and value.	**Customer.** We use two New York banks. **Banker.** May I ask whom you are using? How have you found . . . ? We can provide . . . .
Knowing competitive information.	**Customer.** We use X Bank for our wire transfers. **Banker.** We can provide	Bankers who are familiar with their competitors' products are in a position to ask questions that strike at the competitors' weaknesses. By knowing their own products' capabilities as well as their competitors', bankers can highlight their competitive edge.	**Customer.** We use X Bank for our wire transfers. **Banker.** To what extent do you find that there are delays? [**or**] How long . . . ?

Exhibit 4   Sales Tips (continued)

Area of Possible Difficulty	The Wrong Approach	Analysis	Improvement
Fielding objections.	**Customer.** There are too many errors . . . **Banker.** Not in our system	It is preferable to get specifics before trying to resolve objections and to use the Objection Response Model (repeat, clarify, discuss, check for understanding and agreement) as a way to keep communications open.	**Customer.** There are too many errors. **Banker.** That is a concern, but what specific kinds of errors are you referring to?
Unearthing possible objections.	**Customer.** It sounds fine. **Banker.** Great. I think the Zero-Balance Account could	Bankers should raise a major objection that experience indicates will crop up later, when a customer does not raise it. If there are in fact unexpressed possible concerns or problems, bankers can address them and reinforce the benefits in the customer's mind.	**Customer.** It sounds fine. **Banker.** Great. Let me ask you, how do you think your unit managers will react?

Exhibit 4   Sales Tips (continued)

Area of Possible Difficulty	The Wrong Approach	Analysis	Improvement
Action step with specific closing arrangements.	**Banker.** I'll call you in a week or so.	Initiating and implementing the next step is the responsibility of the banker. A specific time and date should be set at the conclusion of the meeting to facilitate sales actions and reduce the number of "hello calls."	**Banker.** When next week would it be convenient for us to . . . ? 10:30 Tuesday?
	Customer. I'll get back to you in a few days. [or]		That sounds fine. If I don't hear from you by Friday, would it be all right if I contact you to arrange to meet . . . ?
High and wide opportunities— selling to the economic decision maker (high), and the operations or user decision maker (wide).	**Customer.** Let me discuss this with the assistant treasurer. **Banker.** Fine, I'll get back to you.	If a customer refers to a third party who will influence or make the decision, the banker should try to meet with the new contact.	**Customer.** Let me discuss this with the assistant treasurer. **Banker.** That sounds like a good idea. What are your thoughts on my meeting with him [or the two of you] to review . . . ?

Exhibit 4   Sales Tips (continued)

Area of Possible Difficulty	The Wrong Approach	Analysis	Improvement
Joint calls.	**Banker.** I'll have our cash management specialist call you to arrange an appointment.	Bankers, whenever possible, should accompany the specialists, since the primary relationship is with the banker. The banker should arrange the appointment rather than leave it to the specialist or the customer to iniate contact.	**Banker.** I'll arrange an appointment for our cash management specialists to meet with us . . . . When next week . . . ?
Taking notes.	Banker automatically begins to take notes.	It is usually advisable to seek a customer's approval before taking notes.	**Banker.** I'd like to jot down some notes if you don't mind. [**or**] Do you mind if I take these details down?
References to the bank or colleagues.	**Banker.** Those operations people down there . . . . [**or**] I thought they should have accepted the deal. . . .	Bankers should avoid blaming operations, a credit committee, specialists, or management, as a way to defend or explain a problem or a decision. It will reflect negatively on the bank and the banker eventually. It may seem to be an easy out, but bankers may have to pay for it later.	**Banker.** I'm sorry to hear about the problem. Let me check with our operations people . . . . [**or**] We found . . . .

Exhibit 4   Sales Tips (continued)

Area of Possible Difficulty	The Wrong Approach	Analysis	Improvement
Customer sophistication.	**Banker.** Let me explain	Bankers should not make assumptions about a customer's knowledge of a product but rather should enquire how familiar he or she is to avoid being *under* or *over* his or her level. Bankers should take into consideration the position and experience of the customer.	**Banker.** How familiar are you with . . . ? [**or**] What experience have you had with . . . ?
Start-up time.	**Banker.** We can get you started in a week or two.	Bankers should be *realistic* and *co-operate with operations,* but should not unnecessarily extend start-up time, or it can cost the deal. They should take special situations into consideration. Product start-up time must be competitive and efficient.	**Banker.** When would you need the Letter of Credit? **Customer.** I think we would . . . in four days.
Bankerese.	DTC, LCs, ZBAs, ACH, make a market, basis points, and so on.	Bankers should avoid using jargon when discussing a product to avoid confusing customers.	Depository Transfer Check, Letter of Credit, Zero-Balance Account, Automated Clearing House, and so on.

Exhibit 4   Sales Tips (continued)

Area of Possible Difficulty	The Wrong Approach	Analysis	Improvement
Benefits to the customer versus benefits to the bank.	**Banker.** We want to protect your margins, since we have a credit outstanding to you. . . .	Bankers should avoid discussing *benefits to the bank* with a customer. It is preferable to address the product or service as it benefits the *customer.*	**Banker.** We may be able to accelerate the collection of receivables and help reduce your borrowings. . . .

POSSIBLE DIFFICULTIES

Some additional problems that may warrant discussion include the following.

Interrupting the Customer

When the banker and the customer both begin to talk at the same time during the sales interview, the customer *always* has the right of way. Bankers should stop talking and listen. Under no circumstances in a selling situation should bankers interrupt the customer.

Nail Down One Product at a Time

Bankers should complete the action step arrangements for one product before addressing a cross-selling possibility, unless it is a package deal. Nail down one sale at a time, or all opportunities could be lost. For example: Customer is about to sign up for Certificate of Deposit for his or her company; the banker begins to discuss personal investments, which results in drawing attention from and confusing the first almost-made decision.

Seating Arrangements

During a sales call, bankers should select seating that creates an advocate rather than an adversary position when they are given a choice. Right angles, for selling purposes, are always preferable to head-on (directly across from one another) positions.

Range of Products

Bankers should not approach a call prepared to talk to a customer about only one product, unless they have a direct lead. They should be prepared to uncover needs and apply their *range* of product knowledge accordingly. If bankers do their homework, assumptions can be made about product opportunities, but products should be discussed only after needs are identified.

Desk Space

Bankers should avoid putting their paper, coffee, or other items on the customer's desk unless invited to do so. If there is no other option but to use the desk, the banker should ask the customer's permission.

Handouts

Bankers should distribute handouts as they intend to use them, or they may find themselves in competition with the handouts.

Self-Confidence

Confidence is the first and final sales tip. Confidence comes from line success, and success is the result of *preparation* and *practice*. Bankers should do their homework, initiate sales calls, and evaluate their calls and their sales results on an ongoing basis as a way to increase their confidence and effectiveness.

6
Self-Training for Line Bankers

The objective of this book is to accelerate sales effectiveness. Sales training can be addressed in a book, but the integration of the concepts into everyday selling practices must take place *on line*. Although nothing can substitute for experience, the practical and concrete approach to consultative sales presented in this book has been and can be transferred and applied to day-to-day selling situations.

In the final analysis it is the actual day-to-day contact with the customer that determines sales results. Since bankers are frequently on their own when they are making sales calls, it is important that they analyze their sales call activities as a way to measure and improve their sales effectiveness. The first question bankers should ask themselves after a sales interview is "How did it go?" Rather than relying solely on their feelings, bankers should use a concrete set of criteria to understand their feelings and improve their performance. These criteria can also be drawn upon during a sales interview to help them recover *during* an interview that is moving in the wrong direction.

For self-training to work, it should be done with specific sales criteria in a consistent, objective, and organized way. Their self-critique can be most helpful when it is based on specific guidelines, and when an objective set of criteria is used. As a way to assist bankers in applying and integrating the ten elements of a sale into their everyday sales activities, a sales effectiveness checklist has been developed to be used by bankers after each sales call. By using the checklist presented in Exhibit 5 on a daily basis, bankers can evaluate their sales calls, analyze their results, and improve or repeat their sales strategies.

Exhibit 5   Post-Sale   Sales Effectiveness Checklist

Customer: _____ Date of Call: _____

Customer: _____ Prospect: _____

Sales Call Objectives: _____

	Yes	No
Homework		
Was a sales call objective set?	_____	_____
Did the customer qualify as a prospect?	_____	_____
Was the contact with the right decision maker or decision influencer?	_____	_____
Opening		
Was introduction/rapport building effective?	_____	_____
Were sales call objective and possible benefit to customer presented?	_____	_____
Motivation Lever		
Was the customer's present situation system discussed?	_____	_____
Were the customer's needs identified (before product was discussed)?	_____	_____
Were needs satisfied?	_____	_____
Features and Benefits		
Did the product information relate to customer needs?	_____	_____
Was the product knowledge adequate?	_____	_____
Were features linked with customer benefits?	_____	_____
Probing Questions and Incremental Close		
Were probing questions used to find needs and direct the interview?	_____	_____
Were incremental closing used to test for agreement and understanding?	_____	_____
Did the banker listen and incorporate the customer's needs/words?	_____	_____
Was a dialogue developed?	_____	_____
Objections		
Was the Objection Response Model used (repeat, clarify, state features and benefits of product, close incrementally) to resolve objections?	_____	_____
Were objections turned into selling points or offset?	_____	_____

	Yes	No
Competition		
Was competitive information adequate?	___	___
Were competitors identified?	___	___
Was competitive information gathered?	___	___
Were alternatives compared for price and value?	___	___
Total Offer and Pricing		
Was the total relationship taken into consideration?	___	___
Was price related to value?	___	___
Decision Makers		
Were all participants identified prior to the sales call?	___	___
Was there anyone else who should have been included in the meeting?	___	___
Should someone else be contacted or met with before the next meeting?	___	___
Were influences identified and included?	___	___
Action Step		
Were definite next-step arrangements made?	___	___
Were all participants for the next step identified?	___	___
Was information needed for the next step gathered?	___	___
Nonverbal and Sales Environment		
Were the nonverbal signals positive?	___	___
Was the seating arrangement observed and maximized?	___	___
Interpersonal Factors		
Were rapport/relationship established?	___	___
Control		
Did the banker have control of the sales call?	___	___
Sales Call Results		
Was sales call objective met?	___	___

Reader's
Feedback Summary

Based on your sales and banking experience, please supply the following information.

Overall evaluation of the approach to sales in banking presented in this book:

Evaluation of ten elements of a sale:

Areas of the book to be modified or expanded:

Previous experience with sales and product knowledge training in banking:

Additional comments:

Reader's profile
  Position: _____
  Years in banking: _____
  Bank or company: _____
  Division: _____
  Name: _____ (optional)

Kindly return to   John Wiley & Sons, Inc.
                   605 Third Avenue
                   New York, NY 10158

                   Attention: Linda Richardson
                        % Stephen Kippur

Index

Action step, sales interview, 22, 41, 99–101
  closing signals and, 99–100
  closing techniques, 100
  contradictory messages and, 100–101
  initiation of, 99–100
  sales interviews, group presentations, 124
Annual/quarterly report, 131

Bad-experience objections, 83–84
  Objection Response Model, 84
Bankers:
  confidence in, 49–50
  product knowledge and, 10–11, 13
  resistance to selling, 3–4
  role in sales interview, 41–42
  role in selling, 5–7
Bank image objection, 88–89
Banks:
  commercial products, list of, 30–32
  consumer products, list of, 32–34
  see also Sales in banking
Benefits, of a product, 66
Body signals:
  group presentations and, 124
  in sales interview, 101–104
    examples, 102
  supplementing verbal messages, 103–104
  testing body messages, 103
Bridge question:
  example of, 46
  in sales interview, 45–46
  as strategy in opening of sales interview,
    48–49

Brochures, 128–129

Cash management, product profiles, 14
Change, ordeal of change objections, 85–86
Closing, traditional, 95. *See also*
    Action step; Incremental close
Commercial products of banks, 30–32
Competition:
  "asking for the business" and, 97
  example of competitive information, 21
  information about, 20–28
Competitive objections, 80–81
  "my present bank" objection, 81
  "other offer" objection, 80–81
Confidence, 49–50
  in pricing, 77, 79–80
Constructive listening, sales interview, 57–65
  customer's words, use in reply, 62
  disagreement and, 60
  importance of, 58
  for key ideas, 60–61
  negative reply, 62
  note taking, 62
  opportunity phrases, use of, 61
  positive reply, 63
  prior to group presentations, 123
  silence in, 63–65
  technique for, 59–65
Consultative banking, 2–3, 6–7
  banker's skills for, 7
  definition of, 2
  Motivation Lever in, 51, 53
Consumer products, of banks, 32–34

Contacts, decision-makers as, 19
Contracts, 24
Cross-selling, 3, 6, 11
  product-knowledge questions, 29
  relationship of products, 25
Cushion approach, 47
Customer benefit strategy, in sales interview,
    47–48
Customers:
  company knowledge questions, 35
  decision-making units, 19, 125–128
  identifying needs of, 10
  making assumptions about, 36
  Motivation Lever and, 40–51
  motivation, sales interview, 43–44
  multiple, in sales interview, 49
  product knowledge and, 34
  qualifying criteria for products and, 16–19
  representative customers, 19
  sales interview and, 36
  see also Sales interview

Decision-making units, 125–128
  operational staff as, 125, 127
  personnel in, 125
  senior management as, 127
Declining transactions, 113

Features and benefits, sales interview, 65–68
  complementary relationship of, 66–68
  feature-benefit strategy, 65–68
  Import Letter of Credit, example, 67
  sales interview, group presentations, 122
Features, of a product, 66
Feedback, from incremental close, 97–98
Fielding objections, 94
Follow-up, after sales, 23
Foreign Exchange, pricing, 24

Genuine objections, 69
Greeting, in sales interview, 43
Group presentations:
  action step in, 124
  body signals in, 124
  constructive listening in, 123
  developing the presentation, 120–121
  features and benefits in, 122
  incremental close in, 123–124
  monologue for, 116, 117
  necessary prior information, 119–120

objections/responses in, 122
opening in, 121–122
preparation for, 118–120
probing questions in, 123
sales environment and, 124
sales planner for, 126
seating, 120
yellow-pad meetings, 118–121

Handouts, distribution of, 131
Hinge strategy, in sales interview, 48

Image, bank image objection, 88–89
Implementation, of products, 22–23
Import Letter of Credit:
  feature-benefit strategy example, 67
  qualifying criteria, 17
Incremental close, sales interview, 95–99
  action step and, 99–101
  agreement and, 95
  benefits of, 98–99
  difference from traditional close, 95
  examples of, 98
  probing questions in, 96
  reducing rejection, 96–98
  sales interviews, group presentations,
      123–124
Industry experience strategy, in sales
    interview, 48
Inherent objections, 81–83
  examples of, 81–82
  Objection Response Model, 83
Insurmountable objections, 89–90
Interruptions, in sales interview, 107
Introduction, in sales interview, 43

Joint calling, 114–115
  preparation for, 114–115
  tips during the call, 115

Line bankers:
  information to specialists, 25–29
  joint calling, 114
Listening, *see* Constructive listening
Lock Box Services, qualifying criteria, 17–18
Low-key opening, benefit openings, 47–48

Manipulative objections, 90–91
Monologue format, with multiple customers,
    116–117

Motivation Lever, 50–53
  consultative banking and, 51, 53
  customer input, 53
  key questions in, 50
  multiple customers, 116
Multiple customers:
  demands of sales and, 116
  monologue format, 116–117
  opening of sales interview, 49
  sales interview, 116–121
  see also Group presentations

Name-dropping, industry experience strategy, 48
Nonverbal messages, *see* Body signals

Objection Response Model, 70–73
  bad-experience objections, 84
  clarifying questions in, 70–71
  empathy in, 70
  incremental close in, 71
  inherent objections and, 83
  pressure objections, 91
  price objections and, 79
  product information communication, 94
  product knowledge and, 71
  sales opportunities and, 72
  silence in, 72
Objections, in sales interviews, 68–94
  bad-experience objections, 83–84
  bank image objections, 88–89
  communication skills for, 69
  competitive objections, 80–81
  deferral of, 93
  fielding objections, 94
  genuine objections, 69
  group presentations, 122
  inherent objections, 81–83
  insurmountable objections, 89–90
  interviews without objections, 93–94
  manipulative objections, 90–91
  Objection Response Model, 70–73
  ordeal of change objections, 85–86
  premature objections, 90
  price/terms objections, 73–80
  role objections, 69
  as sales opportunities, 68–69, 72, 93
  smoke-screen objections, 86
  turnover objections, 89
  vague objections, 86–88

"what-if" objections, 84
"why" technique, 87–88
Office, in sales interview, 105–106
Opening, sales interview, 42–50
  bridge question in, 45–46
  customer benefit strategy of, 47–48
  greeting in, 43
  group presentations, 121–122
  hinge strategy of, 48
  importance of, 42
  industry experience strategy of, 48
  multiple customers, 49
  professional compliment, strategy of, 48
  question strategy of, 48–49
  rapport building, 43–44
  selling idea of interview, 44–45
  summary in, 44
  third party strategy of, 48
  tone of, 49–50
Operational staff, as decision-making unit, 125, 127
Opportunity phrases:
  examples of, 61
  use in constructive listening, 61–62
Ordeal of change objections, 85–86

Premature objections, 90
Pressure objections, 90–91
Price/term objections, 73–80
  confidence in pricing, 79–80
  cushion approach, 77
  premature price objections, 77–78
  price traps, 73–75
  price trauma, 79
  resistance to price, 73
  Total Offer Approach, 75–77
Pricing, of products, 23–24
Proactive selling, 4
Probing questions, sales interview, 54–57
  definition of, 54
  in incremental close, 96
  multiple questions, 56
  prefacing of, 57
  presentation versus interview format, 57
  problems in questioning, 56–57
  purpose to banker, 56
  sales interviews, group presentations, 123
  silence and, 56
  usefulness of, 55

Product knowledge, 10–37
  action step, 22
  case histories and, 22
  categories of information required, 14–15
  communication skill and, 94
  company knowledge questions, 35
  competitive information, 20–22
  cross-selling and, 25
  customer needs and, 34–36
  customers, developing of, 19
  documentation of sales, 24
  exhibits, 25
  follow-up operational process, 23
  as foundation of selling, 10–11
  identifying customer needs, 10
  implementation process, 22–23
  in-bank contacts and, 24
  information from line to specialists, 25–29
  Objection Response Model and, 94
  objections to products and, 20
  pricing, 23–24
  probing questions and, 20
  "product familes," 25
  product list (commercial products), 30–32
  product list (consumer products), 32–34
  product profiles, 13–19
  questions, 29
  resources for, 12–14
  sales interview and, 36
  sales line, 28
  sales-oriented, 11–12
  sample feedback form, 27
  service catalogue and, 12–13
  start-up time, 21
  types of, 11
Product profiles, 13–19
  categories of information required, 14–15
  description, 15–16
  features and benefits, 16
  qualifying criteria of products, 16–19
Products, benefits and features of, 66
Professional compliment strategy, in sales
        interview, 48

Qualifying criteria:
  considerations for, 18
  for products, 16–19
Question strategy, in sales interview, 48–49.
  See also Probing questions

Rapport building, in sales interview, 43–44
Referrals, third-party, 48
Role objections, 69

Sales:
  consultative, 6, 7
  image of, 4–5
Sales aids, 129
Sales in banking, 2–7
  case example, 2–3
  consultative banking, 2, 6, 7
  cross-selling, 3
  proactive selling, 4
  product knowledge, 10–37
  resistance to, 3–4
  role of bankers, 5–7
Sales environment, in sales interview, 104–107
  continuous interruptions and, 107
  no office and, 105–106
  office in, 105
  sales interviews, group presentations, 124
  seating, 106–107
  time of meeting and, 107
Sales interview, 36
  action step, 99–101
  banker's role, 41–42
  body signals, 101–104
  constructive listening, 57–65
  elements of, 40–41, 108–109
  features and benefits, 65–68
  incremental close, 95–99
  joint calling, 114–115
  Motivation Lever, 50–53
  multiple customers, 116–121
  objections, 68–94
  opening, 42–50
  preparation, 110–115
    focus of, 110
    importance of, 111
    joint calling, 114–115
    outline of, 110
    sales call planner, 112
  probing questions, 54–57
  sales environment, 104–108
Sales materials, 129–132
  annual/quarterly report, 131
  brochures, 128–129
  handouts, distribution of, 131
  maximum effect with, 131–132

sales aids, 129
specification summaries, 130–131
Sales opportunities, objections as, 68–69, 72, 93
Sales-oriented product knowledge, 11–12
Salesperson, image of, 4–5
Sales presentation, multiple customers, 117
Seating:
for group presentations, 120
in sales interview, 106–107
Senior management, as decision-making unit, 127
Service catalogue, 12–13
alternative to, 13–14
problems of, 12–13
Smoke-screen objections, 86
Specialists:
joing calling, 114
referrals by bankers to, 92
Specification summaries, 130–131
Start-up time, for products, 24
Strategies, in opening of sales interview, 47–49

Telephone, declining transactions and, 113
Third-party strategy, in sales interview, 48
Time, in sales interview, 107
Tone, opening of sales interview, 49–50
Total Offer Approach, 75–77
action step and, 101
customer pressure and, 77
elements of, 76–77
parts of, 75
situations for use of, 76
Traditional close, 95
Turnover objection, 89

Vague objections, 86–88

"What-if" objections, 84
"Why" technique, objections and, 87–88

Yellow-pad meetings, 118–121
purpose of, 118–119